VIGO COUNTY PUBLIC LIBRARY
TERRE HAUTE, INDIANA

Vigo Youth Services Juvenile Non–F
39228052712900
973.7 A
Anderson, Maxine
Great Civil War projects

★ ★ ★ ★ ★ ★ ★ ★ ★ ★ ★ ★ ★

GREAT
CIVIL WAR
PROJECTS
You Can Build Yourself

Maxine Anderson

~ Titles in the *Build It Yourself* Series ~

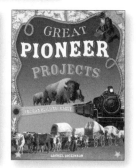

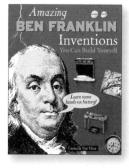

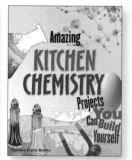

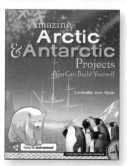

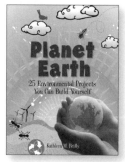

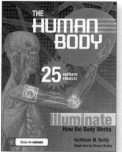

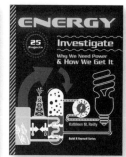

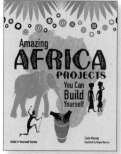

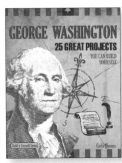

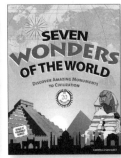

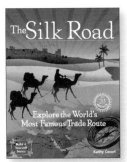

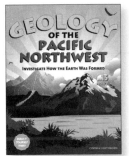

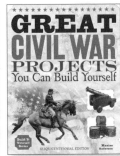

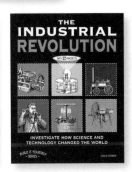

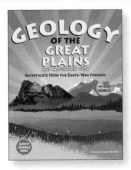

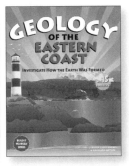

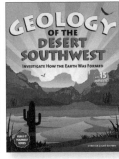

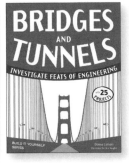

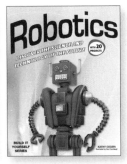

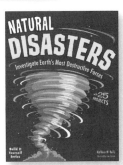

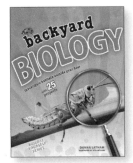

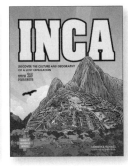

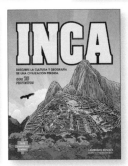

Nomad Press is committed to preserving ancient forests and natural resources. We elected to print *Great Civil War Projects You Can Build Yourself* on 4,007 lbs. of Williamsburg Recycled 30% offset.

Nomad Press made this paper choice because our printer, Sheridan Books, is a member of Green Press Initiative, a nonprofit program dedicated to supporting authors, publishers, and suppliers in their efforts to reduce their use of fiber obtained from endangered forests.

For more information, visit **www.greenpressinitiative.org**

Nomad Press
A division of Nomad Communications
10 9 8 7 6 5 4 3 2 1

Copyright © 2012 by Nomad Press. All rights reserved.
No part of this book may be reproduced in any form without permission in writing from the publisher, except by a reviewer who may quote brief passages in a review or **for limited educational use**.
The trademark "Nomad Press" and the Nomad Press logo are trademarks of Nomad Communications, Inc.

This book was manufactured by Sheridan Books,
Ann Arbor, MI USA.
April 2012, Job # 334839
ISBN: 978-1-936749-45-4

Educational Consultant Marla Conn

Questions regarding the ordering of this book should be addressed to
Independent Publishers Group
814 N. Franklin St.
Chicago, IL 60610
www.ipgbook.com

Nomad Press
2456 Christian St.
White River Junction, VT 05001
www.nomadpress.net

Contents

★ ★ ★ ★ ★ CIVIL WAR TIMELINE ★ ★ ★ ★ ★

November 1860: Abraham Lincoln is elected President of the United States. Lincoln is against the spread of slavery to new territories in America, and many southern states think he is a threat to their way of life.

December 1860: South Carolina secedes from the Union.

Early 1861: Six more southern states, Mississippi, Alabama, Florida, Georgia, Texas, and Louisiana, secede from the United States of America. They form a new country with its own government and constitution called the Confederate States of America. Jefferson Davis is named its president.

April 1861: Confederate soldiers capture Fort Sumter in South Carolina from the Union. This starts the Civil War and leads Virginia, North Carolina, Arkansas, and Tennessee to secede from the Union and join the Confederacy. Richmond, Virginia, is named the new capital.

July 1861: In the first major conflict in the Civil War, called the First Battle of Bull Run or the First Battle of Manassas, the Union army is forced to retreat northward toward Washington, D.C.

Fall 1861: The Union navy blockades the coastline of the Confederate states to cut off their supplies.

May 1862: Confederate General Stonewall Jackson and his troops battle Union forces in the Shenandoah Valley in Virginia. They force the Union soldiers to retreat across the Potomac River to Washington, D.C.

August 1862: The Second Battle of Bull Run, or the Second Battle of Manassas, is a victory for the Confederacy.

September 1862: Harper's Ferry falls to Confederate troops under the command of General Jackson, leading to the Battle of Antietam. This is known as the bloodiest day of the war, although there is no clear winner.

January 1863: President Lincoln issues the Emancipation Proclamation, freeing all slaves in the Confederacy.

May 1863: At the Battle of Chancellorsville, Virginia, the Confederates win a major victory under General Robert E. Lee. The victory is ruined when General Stonewall Jackson dies from his wounds a few days later.

July 1863: The Gettysburg Campaign is the turning point of the war, with huge Confederate losses. At the same time Confederates surrender Vicksburg, Mississippi, to General Ulysses S. Grant of the Union army. This puts much of the Mississippi River under the control of the Union army and splits the Confederacy in half.

September 1863: Confederates win the Battle of Chickamauga, Georgia.

November 1863: In the Battle of Chattanooga, Union soldiers take control of the city and then almost all of Tennessee. Lincoln delivers his famous Gettysburg Address at a ceremony dedicating a soldiers' cemetery at the site of the Battle of Gettysburg. It begins with the lines, "Four score and seven years ago our fathers brought forth, upon this continent, a new nation, conceived in liberty, and dedicated to the proposition that all men are created equal."

May–June 1864: General Grant leads the Wilderness Campaign, a long and bloody battle. He pursues General Lee's soldiers relentlessly toward Richmond, despite enormous casualties.

August–November 1864: Union General William T. Sherman marches from Chattanooga, Tennessee, to Atlanta, Georgia, taking the city and continuing to the sea. Abraham Lincoln is re-elected to another term.

January 1865: The United States Congress approves the Thirteenth Amendment to the United States Constitution, abolishing slavery.

April 1865: The Confederate capitol of Richmond, Virginia, falls to Union forces. General Lee surrenders. Less than one week later President Lincoln is shot and killed by John Wilkes Booth.

May 1865: Remaining Confederate troops surrender and Jefferson Davis, president of the Confederate States of America, is captured in Georgia.

THE UNION

Abraham Lincoln: President of the United States from 1861 to 1865. Lincoln won the election of 1860 with less than 40 percent of the popular vote, and his election prompted the secession of the southern states. Lincoln's Emancipation Proclamation in 1863 freed slaves in territories held by the Confederacy, and he is famous today as the president who ended slavery in the United States. He was assassinated by John Wilkes Booth on April 14, 1865.

Ulysses S. Grant: Commander of the Union forces in 1864. Grant was an army officer who left the service in 1854, then rejoined at the start of the Civil War. No one expected very much of him, but he led his troops to several stunning victories on the western front. After taking command of the Union forces Grant was able to defeat the Confederates in less than a year.

THE CONFEDERACY

Jefferson Davis: President of the Confederate States from 1861 to 1865. Davis had been a U.S. senator for many years, and he was President Franklin Pierce's secretary of war from 1853 to 1857. He joined the Confederacy hoping for a military command, and was instead elected president by the Confederate Congress. After the Confederacy lost the war Davis spent two years in prison on charges of treason. He died in 1899.

Robert E. Lee: Commander of the Army of Northern Virginia, the leading Confederate army. Lee was asked by President Lincoln in 1861 to command the Union army. He declined, and instead took command of the Confederate forces. Robert E. Lee was universally liked and respected by both Confederate and Union leaders.

INTRODUCTION

*H*ave you ever wondered what life was like during the **Civil War**? A lot depended on the color of your skin, where you lived, and if you were rich or poor before the Civil War started. But whether you lived in the Deep South or the Far North, whether your hometown was the site of a battle or far away from any fighting, you would have been affected by the war between the **Union** and **Confederate** armies.

This book will help you discover what life was like during the Civil War for families, soldiers, and children. You'll learn why the Civil War began. You'll find some interesting facts about the people, places, and battles during the war. And you'll create projects that will give you an idea of how people communicated, had fun, and lived their day-to-day lives during the Civil War.

WORDS 2 KNOW

Civil War: the war in the United States, from 1861 to 1865, between the states in the North and the slave-owning states in the South.

Union: the United States, but especially the northern states during the American Civil War.

Confederate: the government established by the southern states of the United States after they left the Union in 1860 and 1861. Called the Confederate States of America or the Confederacy.

The book is divided into two general sections, *On The Battlefield* deals with a soldier's life in camp and during battle. *On The Homefront* gives you an idea of what life was like for everyday people during the Civil War. Most of the projects in this book can be made with minimal adult supervision, and the supplies needed are either common household items or easily available at craft stores. So, take a step back into the 1860s and get ready to *Build It Yourself.*

Confederate flag.

Union flag.

HOW IT ALL BEGAN

The Civil War, also called the War Between the States, officially began on April 12, 1861. The Confederate army attacked Fort Sumter in South Carolina, which belonged to the Union. Within two days, the Union soldiers surrendered the fort to the Confederacy. This was the first battle of a war that lasted four years and cost more than half a million lives. But the reason for the war started much earlier.

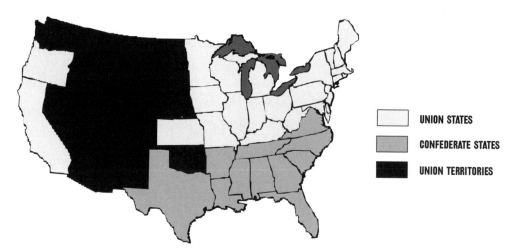

☐ UNION STATES
▨ CONFEDERATE STATES
■ UNION TERRITORIES

Some would say the Civil War began as far back as the founding of the United States, almost 100 years before those first shots were fired.

So what was the cause of the war? **Slavery**. When the founders of the United States wrote the **Constitution** in 1787, they included some rules about slavery. This was because slavery was an important part of **plantation** life in the South. The founders of the country realized they would need to allow slavery to continue there, or the leaders of the South would not agree to the Constitution as the law of the land.

In states where slavery was legal when the Constitution was written, slavery would remain legal. It was agreed that the **slave trade** could continue until 1808. It was also agreed that a slave could not become free by escaping to another state. But what happened when a new state wanted to join the Union? The people voting would have to decide for themselves whether to allow slavery in their new state.

WORDS 2 KNOW

slavery: when slaves are used as workers. A slave is a person owned by another person and forced to work, without pay, against their will.

Constitution: the document that sets up the rules for how our country is governed.

plantation: a large farm in the South with slaves for workers.

slave trade: buying people in Africa to sell in America.

federal territory: land belonging to the United States that was not yet a state.

Louisiana Purchase: land west of the Mississippi River that the United States bought from France in 1803.

Every time a new state entered the Union, there was another fight about slavery.

Compromises were made so the balance of free states and slave states stayed equal. The Missouri Compromise in 1820 brought Missouri into the Union as a slave state, and Maine into the Union as a free state. The Missouri Compromise also made it illegal to have slaves in **federal territory** that was part of the **Louisiana Purchase** north of a line that formed Missouri's southern border.

WORDS 2 KNOW

fugitive: someone who escapes or runs away.

prohibit: to make illegal.

abolish: to end something.

fertile: good for growing crops.

The Compromise of 1850 brought California into the Union as a free state, but also passed a new and stronger **Fugitive** Slave Act. This law declared that runaway slaves found in any state had to be returned to their owners.

The situation was balanced, but no one was very happy with it.

An 1857 decision by the United States Supreme Court, called the Dred Scott decision, made the situation even worse. At the time, the United States was the same size as it is today, but had only 31 states. Most of the land in the middle and western half of the country was divided into territories. The Dred Scott decision ruled that no one—not Congress or any territorial government—could **prohibit** or **abolish** slavery in any federal territory. This meant that a slave owner could bring slaves to a federal territory and legally own them there, even if the territory was considered a "free territory."

Slave auction.

Many southern planters wanted to expand the cotton industry to new, **fertile** soil in the western territories. But the northern states wanted to prohibit slavery there to keep the balance equal between slave and free states.

THE BRINK OF WAR

The slave state–free state **issue** became violent when the Kansas territory was choosing whether to enter the Union as a free state or a slave state. People from outside Kansas tried to influence the vote. The territory became known as "Bleeding Kansas" because of the bloody battles between people who supported Kansas as a slave state and people who supported Kansas as a free state. In 1861, Kansas voted to become a free state. At that point the entire country was on the brink of war with itself.

WORDS 2 KNOW

issue: subject of concern.

secede: to leave, or formally withdraw.

By the presidential election of 1860, the southern states were ready to split from the Union.

The southern states didn't want to be part of a Union where a central government made all the rules. Each state in the South wanted to keep slavery legal. Southern states were sure Abraham Lincoln was anti-slavery. They believed he would restrict slavery in new states as the first step toward its "ultimate extinction," as Lincoln once put it, if he were elected.

Abraham Lincoln

A month after Lincoln won the election in November 1860, South Carolina **seceded** from the United States. Florida, Mississippi, Alabama, Louisiana, Georgia, and Texas joined South Carolina to form a new country, the Confederate States of America. They were soon joined by Virginia, Tennessee, Missouri, and Kentucky. Jefferson Davis was elected as its president on February 4, 1861. Two months later, the first shots of the Civil War were fired.

ON THE BATTLEFIELD

ost soldiers who joined up to fight for either the Union or the Confederacy had no idea what they were getting into. Why did soldiers join? In the case of the Confederacy, most wanted to defend their state, their home, and their families. Most of the fighting took place in the southern half of the country, in the states that had seceded.

"Clear the Track—Union For Ever"
pictorial envelope.

Union soldiers joined up for a variety of reasons. Some believed in the idea of a single country and a national government. Some believed in the **abolitionist** cause. Others were looking for adventure.

Soldiers on both sides found that they spent far more time waiting around camp or marching long distances than they did fighting on the battlefield. When they did fight, it was slaughter on a massive scale. In the Battle of Gettysburg, more than 51,000 men were killed or wounded in three days.

Even more soldiers died of disease than of battle wounds. For every soldier killed in battle, two died of diseases such as dysentery, diarrhea, typhoid, and malaria. This was mostly due to the crowded and unhealthy living conditions. Soldiers from rural areas contracted childhood diseases such as measles and chickenpox because they'd never had them before. More than 5,000 Union soldiers died of measles during the war.

Battlefield medicine was very basic. No one sterilized instruments or operating areas. Also, ammunition called the "minie" ball shattered bones and infected wounds with clothing and dirt. The most common method of treating leg or arm wounds was to **amputate** as soon as possible. In total, more than 200,000 men died of battle wounds, usually from shock and infection.

These injuries led the Union and Confederate armies to change the way they waged war. New weapons shot much farther and more accurately than ever before. By the end of the war, **siege fighting** had taken the place of close-range fighting.

WORDS 2 KNOW

abolitionist: someone who believed that slavery should be abolished, or ended.

amputate: to cut off.

siege fighting: long battles where each side digs in and waits for the other side to surrender.

Zouave ambulance crew demonstrating removal of wounded soldiers from the field.

Siege Fighting

In earlier wars, battles were fought at close hand and victories and defeats were quick and decisive. New weapons developed during the Civil War changed the methods of battle to siege fighting. Battles lasted for long periods of time—sometimes as long as several months. **Troops** often dug trenches and fortifications in the ground and stayed in them, fighting only from time to time and waiting for the other side to quit.

WORDS 2 KNOW

troops: large groups of soldiers.

sutler: someone who sells food and supplies to an army.

draft: a system where people have to join an army.

Camp life was boring. Soldiers spent time drilling (marching in formation), mounting up (preparing to move into battle), and working around camp. For Union soldiers, food and other supplies were easily available. What they weren't assigned they could usually buy at the nearby **sutler's** wagons. Confederate soldiers had far fewer supplies. They often depended on the generosity of family members or nearby farmers and businesses.

Civil War soldiers rarely went home. Most had signed up for three months, but as the war dragged on, they re-upped for periods of up to three years. About a year into the war the Confederates created a **draft**, and a year later, the Union did, too. When the war finally ended in 1865, more than a million men and boys had been killed or wounded. The South was in ruins.

Soldiers pass the time playing dominoes at a mess table.

BANDS AND MUSIC

Music was important in the lives of Civil War soldiers, both on and off the battlefield. A military band always played at **recruitment rallies**, and most volunteer **regiments** joined up with a complete band of their own. The bands helped boost soldier morale during long marches, entertained them in camp, and inspired them before and during battles.

The most common instruments that were played in bands during the war were drums and bugles, and sometimes fifes. **Cavalry** and **artillery** units only used bugles. The **infantry** used fifes as well. The bugler was also responsible for signaling on the battlefield. Individual regiments could distinguish their own bugler's calls from the bugle calls of other regiments.

WORDS 2 KNOW

recruitment rally: a public gathering to add new members to an army.

regiment: a large group of soldiers divided into smaller groups, called battalions.

cavalry: soldiers trained to fight on horseback.

artillery: a division of the army that handles large weapons.

infantry: soldiers trained to fight on foot.

Civil War band.

Why were drummers vital for battlefield communication? The type of weapons used in the war created huge amounts of smoke, so soldiers couldn't see well. Drummers helped soldiers locate their units and helped keep the units together. Drums were often the best way to signal troops on the battlefield, since the noise of battle often drowned out the sound of voices. When soldiers heard a long drum roll, they knew that this was a signal to march into combat. Off the battlefield or at camp, three single drumbeats signaled the end of a soldier's day.

KNOW YOUR CIVIL WAR SLANG

here's your mule—a term the infantry used to insult the cavalry.

web feet—a term the cavalry used to insult the infantry.

Battle of the Bands

Often at sunset, regimental bands on both sides played songs back and forth to each other, matching each other's playing of a particular song. They started with marching music and popular songs, and as the evening wore on, they played softer, slower songs.

In December 1862, a couple of weeks after the Battle of Fredericksburg, one of the bloodiest battles of the war, 100,000 Union troops and 70,000 Confederate troops were camped on opposite sides of the Rappahannock River. The regimental bands were playing their usual evening rounds of songs. As the evening wore on, one of the Union bands started playing "Home, Sweet Home." One by one all the other regimental bands joined in. All other activity in the camps stopped, and all 170,000 men were silent as they listened to the bands play the song.

When the song finally ended, there was a moment of silence, and then suddenly both sides started cheering. One soldier wrote, "Had there not been a river between them, the two armies would have met face to face, shaken hands, and ended the war on that spot."

Drum Corps of Sixty-First New York Infantry.

As the armies changed tactics to siege fighting, **trench warfare**, and units that were smaller and quicker, they used buglers more and drummers less. Over time, the weapons on the battlefield became more powerful and much louder than at any other time in history, making the drums hard to hear.

WORDS 2 KNOW

trench warfare: when opposing troops fight from ditches facing each other.

Bugler.

Most of the drummers and buglers in the Civil War were boys, sometimes as young as 11 years old. While each side banned boys from fighting, a boy could join the army as a drummer or bugler. They were "nonfighting" positions so recruiters let them sign on without questioning their age. Since most people didn't even have birth certificates, sneaking into the army on either side wasn't very difficult.

∽ CIVIL WAR FACTS & TRIVIA ∽

★ One Union drummer named Orion Howe, who was 14 years old, won the Medal of Honor. This medal was first given out in the Civil War. He had relayed orders on the battlefield even though he was terribly wounded.

★ The Union army had more than 40,000 drummers and buglers. The Confederates had 20,000.

★ Musicians also served as stretcher bearers. When battles were over the band members carried the wounded off the battlefield.

One of the most famous boy soldiers in the Civil War was a drummer named Johnny Clem. He first tried to join the Union army when he was nine, but was turned down. So he ran away from home and attached himself to the Twenty-Second Michigan Infantry Unit. The soldiers in the unit liked him, so they let him stay.

Johnny Clem did errands around camp for the soldiers, and they taught him how to be a drummer boy. During the Battle of Shiloh, a shell ripped through his drum, and Johnny Clem was given the nickname Johnny Shiloh. In 1863 the army finally allowed him to enlist, and he rose to the rank of general before his career was over.

John Lincoln Clem, nicknamed Johnny Shiloh, age 12, 1863.

KNOW YOUR CIVIL WAR SLANG

fit as a fiddle—in good shape, healthy, feeling good.

CIVIL WAR BUGLE

1 Have an adult help you cut about 2 feet (⅔ meter) off the nozzle end of the garden hose, keeping the nozzle part on. The nozzle will be your mouthpiece.

2 Coil the hose into one loop with the mouthpiece at one end and the cut end at the other. Duct tape the coil together.

3 Put the funnel in the cut end of the hose. If it is too wide to fit inside the hose, you can duct tape it to the end of the hose.

4 To play your garden hose–bugle (or any brass instrument), you'll need to press your lips together and make a buzzing noise against the mouthpiece. This takes a little practice, but by changing the shape of your mouth while buzzing you can make a lot of different notes. You can even play "Taps." Of course, it won't sound as good as a regular bugle, but the notes will work.

Music for Taps:

GGC GCE GCE
GCE GCE CEG
ECG GGC

SUPPLIES

- **garden hose** (make sure it's okay with your parents to cut up, or buy a cheap hose at any discount store)
- **garden shears or a sharp knife**
- **duct tape**
- **kitchen funnel**

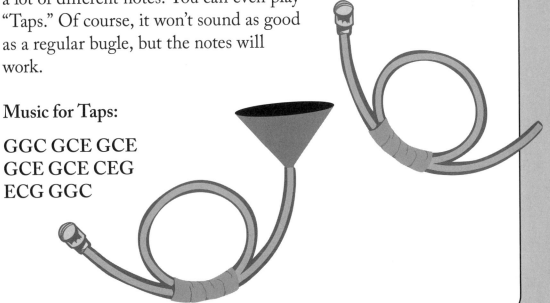

CIVIL WAR DRUM

1 Cut off the top and bottom of your cylindrical container.

2 Decorate your paper the way you want the outside of the drum to look. During the Civil War, drums were usually stained brown on the outside and often decorated with a pattern.

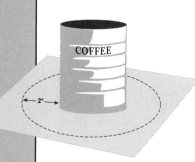

3 Use tape or glue to attach your decorated paper to the container. Cut the paper to fit if needed.

4 Take your chosen material for the top and bottom and cut out circular pieces. The pieces should be large enough that an inch or two of material hangs over the edge of the container. During the Civil War, this material would be calfskin, which stretches easily and is sensitive to moisture.

SUPPLIES

- **cylindrical container** like a coffee can, oatmeal box, or nut container—different containers will make different pitches
- **can opener or scissors**
- **piece of paper** to wrap around your container
- **coloring/decorating materials**
- **tape or glue**
- **canvas, rubber material, or leather** large enough to cover the top and bottom of the container
- **2 large rubber bands**
- **wooden spoons, sticks, wooden rods, pencils, or pens** for drumsticks

5 Use the rubber bands to hold the material around the container. Pull the material tight all around so the drum will beat well.

6 You can glue pieces of string or draw dark lines from the top to the bottom in a zigzag fashion, creating triangles or parallel lines on the outside of the drum. Civil War drums had these lines made with brown or black rope.

7 Now that your drum is complete, play it using your drumsticks. Experiment with different beats and striking the drum in the center or at the edges. You can hear what Civil War musicians sounded like at youtube.com. Have an adult help you search for "Civil War drum calls" or "Civil War music."

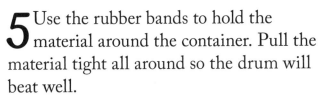

A possible way to decorate your drum.

ON THE BATTLEFIELD
PHOTOGRAPHY

The Civil War was the first time in American history that photography was used to make a public record of events. Up to then, artists sketched events. The art of photography was only 21 years old when the Civil War started, but it was already quite popular in the United States. Before leaving for the war, many Civil War soldiers had their

Ambrotype of a Civil War soldier.

portraits taken. Traveling photographers or small photography studios used a type of photography known as ambrotype. These were one-of-a-kind images made on glass or metal.

Civil War–era photographer.

Photographers also traveled to camps and battlegrounds, recording the events of the war. Most of these photographs used a wet-plate negative. A glass plate was chemically treated, then exposed to the image for five to 30 seconds. This created a negative that could be printed on paper many times.

Mathew Brady

Mathew Brady

The most famous photographer of the Civil War was Mathew Brady, a portrait photographer in New York before the war. Brady photographed many important political leaders in his studio and was one of the first to use photographs as a way to record historical events.

When the Civil War broke out, Brady recruited a group of photographers to travel throughout the United States, making a photographic record of the battles, soldiers, and cities affected by the war. Brady didn't take many of the photographs himself, but every photograph taken by his assistants was credited, "Photo by Brady," making him famous during the war. He also bought many negatives of war images taken by independent photographers. More than 5,000 images were taken during the Civil War, many of them credited to Mathew Brady.

In 1875, Congress paid Brady $27,840 for the rights to all of his images. Brady died in 1895, and was buried in Arlington National Cemetery to honor him for his important photographic work during the war.

Civil War photographers did not go on the battlefield during fighting. Photographic equipment was bulky and delicate, and the process of exposing and developing the images made it almost impossible to take action shots. This meant photographers had to photograph the battlefield after fighting had ended, often before wounded or dead soldiers could be moved to field hospitals.

KNOW YOUR CIVIL WAR SLANG

somebody's darling—a dead soldier. Also the name of a popular Civil War song.

Field photographers sometimes rearranged dead bodies on the battlefield to make their shots look more dramatic.

∽ CIVIL WAR FACTS & TRIVIA ∽

★ Timothy O'Sullivan, one of Mathew Brady's field photographers, took dramatic images of the Battle of Gettysburg. These images inspired Abraham Lincoln's famous Gettysburg Address at the dedication of the Soldier's National Cemetery at Gettysburg. President Lincoln used the Gettysburg Address to emphasize the idea that all men are created equal.

★ Civil War photographer **reenactors** use the art of wet-plate photography. They make photographs of **reenactments** in the same way Civil War photographers made their originals.

★ Of the thousands of photographs taken during the Civil War, not one is of an actual battle in progress.

WORDS 2 KNOW

reenactor: someone who acts out a past event.

reenactment: acting out a past event.

Civil War–era photographer's wagon.

PINHOLE CAMERA

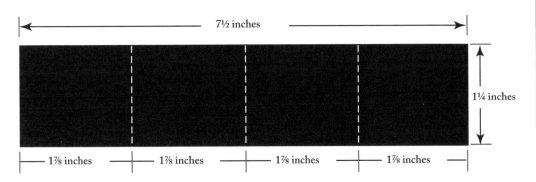

7½ inches

1¼ inches

1⅞ inches — 1⅞ inches — 1⅞ inches — 1⅞ inches

1 Measure and cut the cardboard to 7½ inches in length and 1¼ inches in width (18¾ by 3 centimeters). Then mark four equal sections of 1⅞ inches in width (see diagram) (4¾ centimeters). Use a knife to cut the cardboard slightly (not all the way through) so that it's easier to fold. Fold the cardboard into a box, and tape it with black tape. The inside must be black, so use the black paper to make a lining for the inside of your box. You can also paint it black.

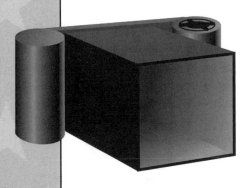

2 Insert the box into the film cartridge, with one of the open sides of the box toward the film cartridge (so that the film cartridge creates a fifth side of the cube). This should be a snug fit.

SUPPLIES

- ruler
- thick corrugated cardboard
- scissors
- pencil
- knife
- black tape
- black paper or black paint
- film—one cartridge of 110 size color film, such as Kodak Gold 200
- aluminum foil
- pin (must be straight) or sewing needle
- two large rubber bands
- dime or nickel

CONTINUES ON NEXT PAGE . . .

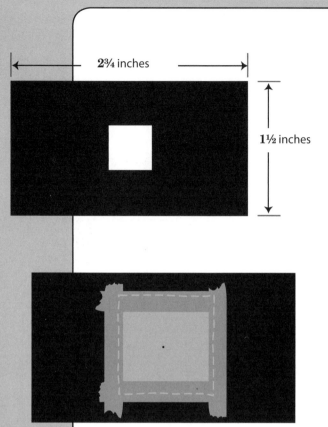

2¾ inches

1½ inches

3 To create the front of the camera, cut another rectangle of cardboard, 2¾ inches by 1½ inches (7 by 3¾ centimeters). Line this piece with black paper or paint it black. Cut a square hole ½ inch by ½ inch (1¼ by 1¼ centimeters) in the center of this piece of cardboard and tape a 1-inch square of aluminum foil over the hole (2½ centimeters). Punch a small hole in the foil with the pin, being careful to make it as small as possible.

4 Fasten the front of the camera to the rest of the camera with two strong rubber bands (see diagram).

5 Make sure that no light is leaking into your camera from the sides or the top or bottom. Use black tape to cover any holes or gaps.

6 When you aren't taking a picture, the pinhole must be covered by a piece of black paper. This can be done by taping paper over the hole or creating some kind of shutter that slides across the hole.

7 Use the dime or nickel to advance the film, turning in a counterclockwise direction. There is a small window on the side of the film cartridge that will indicate the advancing of the film. The film will be in proper position when the numbers 3 and 4 show up in the window.

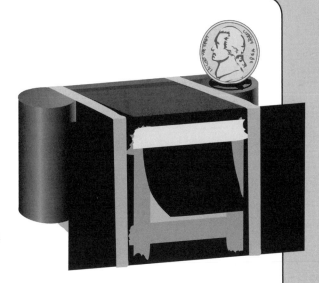

HOW TO TAKE A PICTURE

1 Make sure that the camera is very stable. The best pictures will be produced when the camera doesn't move when the film is being exposed. You can set it on a solid surface such as a chair, table, windowsill, or rock. The pinhole opening should face what you are photographing.

2 Experiment with different exposure times. This is how long you let light into the pinhole. One to three seconds should work, but depending on the amount of sun or light that is available, this time may change.

3 Don't forget to cover the pinhole with black paper after each exposure.

4 If you want to ensure that you get a decent image, you may want to take your picture two or three times with different exposure times. The technique of taking three exposures—one with the recommended exposure time, one with twice the time, and one with half the time—is called bracketing.

FLAGS OF THE CIVIL WAR

*F*lags played an important role during the Civil War. Called "colors," they were the symbols of Union **sympathizers** versus Confederate sympathizers. Flags flew above forts, letting people know what group the fort belonged to, and they were carried during battle.

Regimental flags, which were flags representing different groups of soldiers, helped to keep the group together on the battlefield. Confederate regiments usually carried a flag with a design that corresponded to their armies. If a regiment was in the Army of Northern Virginia, for example, its flag was usually a red square with a Confederate cross of blue stripes and white stars.

WORDS 2 KNOW

sympathizer: a person who agrees with an opinion or a side of an issue.

Washington, D.C. Signal Corps officers lowering the flag at their camp near Georgetown.

The Color Guard

One of the most important jobs a soldier could have was to be part of a regiment's Color Guard—the group of men who carried the colors into battle. Men chosen for the Color Guard were appointed because of bravery or service to their unit. To be chosen for this honor was equal to receiving a medal.

Members of the Color Guard were excused from regular camp duty, but they were expected to lead their regiment into every battle. Their job was to protect the flag bearer, known as the color sergeant, who was constantly in grave danger. This was the most dangerous job during the Civil War. If the color sergeant fell and the enemy captured the flag, it was a great victory for the flag capturers and a terrible loss for the regiment.

Individual regiments put their regiment number and the initials of their home state on their flag. Some regiments also added the names of the battles they had fought. Union regimental flags and Confederate regimental flags were often very decorated.

It is said that the more regimental colors an army was flying, the greater its strength.

In addition to regimental flags, there were artillery, cavalry, engineer, and hospital flags. Flags were also used as post offices: if a commander needed to get a message to another officer on the battlefield, he could send a rider to the regiment's flag and find the officer nearby.

THE UNION'S FORT SUMTER FLAG

This flag flew at Fort Sumter when Union troops resided there early in 1861. There were 33 stars on the Union flag, representing the 33 states in the Union at that time. Today we have 50 states.

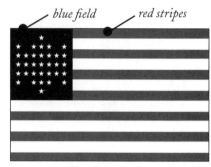
Fort Sumter flag.

On April 11, 1861, Major Robert Anderson, the man in charge of the Union troops, was told by General Beauregard of the Confederate army to **evacuate** the fort. Anderson refused to leave. Confederate **forces** in Charleston, South Carolina, attacked Fort Sumter, marking the beginning of the Civil War.

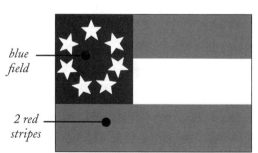

evacuate: to leave a dangerous place to go to a safe place.

forces: a military group organized to fight.

The Confederate troops launched their attack in the early morning hours of April 12. By April 13, the Union flag had been fired upon and shot down, and the fort was on fire. The Confederates, seeing the flag lowered, believed this meant surrender. As they were rowing a boat over to the fort to evacuate the Union troops, Anderson raised another flag, indicating to the Confederates that this battle was not yet over. It took two more attacks by the Confederates to weaken Anderson and his troops enough to force their surrender.

"Stars and Bars," the first Confederate flag, adopted March 1861.

On April 14, the Union flag was lowered and the Confederate palmetto flag was raised.

Fort Sumter with Confederate "stars and bars" colors flying.

PALMETTO FLAG OF SOUTH CAROLINA

The palmetto flag is named for the central emblem, a palmetto tree. This is the South Carolina state tree, and was credited with protecting a South Carolina fort in an attack by the British in 1776. The wood was so strong that the cannonballs fired from the British ships could not destroy the fort, and very few people were injured or killed. The palmetto flag remains South Carolina's state flag today.

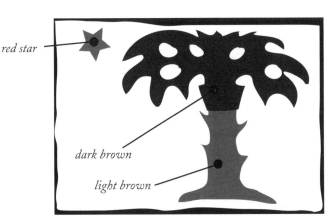

Palmetto flag.

THE CALIFORNIA 100

The California 100 was a group of about 100 men from California who were originally from the East Coast. This group wanted to join the Union forces in the East. They contacted the governor of Massachusetts in the summer of 1862 and asked for permission to join a new cavalry regiment being formed in Massachusetts.

The governor allowed them to join under the condition that they have their own uniform, flag, and equipment. The group agreed and became officially known as Company A of the Second Massachusetts Cavalry. They were popularly referred to as the "California 100."

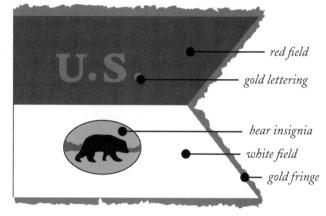

red field

gold lettering

bear insignia

white field

gold fringe

California 100 flag.

KNOW YOUR CIVIL WAR SLANG

. . . .

fresh fish—new recruits.

. . . .

duds—clothing.

. . . .

hayfoot, strawfoot—command used to teach new soldiers the difference between left (hayfoot) and right (strawfoot).

The California 100 carried a flag with a bear on it. This bear now flies on the California state flag.

To get to Massachusetts, the group sailed all the way down the West Coast from San Francisco to Panama, then up the East Coast to Boston. The California 100 was so successful that many more volunteers from California signed up to fight for the Union. They were a separate company at first, but later joined with the California 100.

HOSPITAL FLAG

Hospital flags were created to signal to wounded soldiers that help was nearby. Field hospitals were usually set up in tents behind the battlefield or in a nearby barn. This allowed wounded soldiers to have quick access to medical attention.

The original hospital flag was red, but it created confusion with the red Confederate flag. In 1862, the hospital flag was redesigned as a large, yellow flag. Later it was made more distinctive by the addition of a green "H" in the center of the flag. A smaller yellow flag with a green border was used to mark the quickest route to the hospital.

KNOW YOUR CIVIL WAR SLANG

hospital rat—a person who fakes illness.

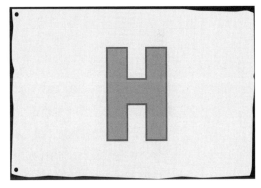

Hospital flag.

Hospital tents behind Douglas Hospital, Washington, D.C., May 1864.

UNION FORT SUMTER FLAG

1 Cut the pillowcase in half and use one side of it. Save the other to make a different flag.

SUPPLIES

- **old pillowcase** or other material of any light color
- **scissors**
- **markers, fabric paint, or fabric** in red, white, and blue
- **paintbrush**
- **adhesive/fabric glue**
- **wooden dowel**

2 Use the diagram provided below to help you sketch and color the features of the flag. Notice that the stars were in a different configuration than they are today.

3 Attach your flag to the wooden dowel or hang it wherever and however you'd like.

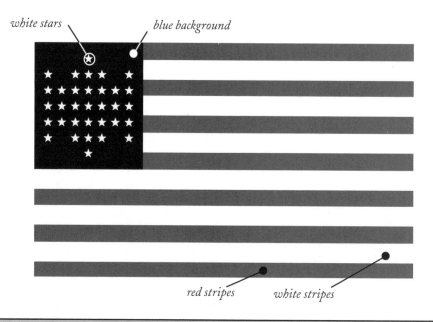

white stars   *blue background*

red stripes   *white stripes*

IRONCLAD SHIPS

When Virginia seceded from the Union in 1861, it took an important **asset** with it: the Union's shipyard in Portsmouth, Virginia. This was valuable to the Confederacy, since almost all of the shipyards were located in the Union's northeastern states.

WORDS 2 KNOW

asset: something useful or valuable.

fleet: a group of ships.

USS Merrimack *(1856–1861)*.

It was also a serious loss to the Union. The Portsmouth Shipyard was where much of the Union's **fleet** was repaired. In addition, everything at the shipyard became the property of the Confederate army, including the USS *Merrimack*, one of the Union navy's biggest and most powerful ships.

KNOW YOUR CIVIL WAR SLANG

opening of the ball—units
waiting to move into battle.

Union sailors burned everything they could before they left the shipyard, including the *Merrimack*. But the ship sank to the river bottom while it was burning, and so it only burned down to the deck. The Confederates dredged the ship up from the river and discovered that it was still usable. They decided to try something new: to build a ship covered in iron so that cannonballs and shells would bounce off the sides rather than smash them to pieces.

The Confederates built a new structure on top of the ship's deck with wooden sides 2 feet thick. On top of that, they lay two layers of 2-inch-thick iron (5 centimeters). Ten cannons were placed inside the ship, their barrels sticking out of narrow openings in the iron-covered sides. One soldier described the ship as looking "like the roof of a very big barn belching forth smoke as from a chimney on fire."

CSS Virginia *(1862-1862), wash drawing by Clary Ray, 1898.*

The Confederates renamed their new ship the *Virginia*. They planned to attack the Union warships in the waters off Norfolk, Virginia, then steam up the Potomac River and attack Washington, D.C.

Upon hearing about the Confederate ironclad ship,
the Union set to work on its own ironclad.
In only 100 days, the Union built the **Monitor,**
a ship that changed the face of naval warfare forever.

The *Monitor* was unlike any ship ever made, described as a cheese box on a raft. It was very slow in the water. But what made the *Monitor* so remarkable was its revolving cannon **turret**. The turret could be turned 360 degrees, so that the two cannons inside could fire in any direction. In contrast, the *Virginia's* cannons could only be fired when the ship was facing its target.

WORDS 2 KNOW

turret: a small tower for guns or other weapons.

USS Monitor, *published in* Harper's Weekly, *March 22, 1862.*

On March 8, 1862, the *Virginia* attacked the Union fleet in the waters of Hampton Roads, Virginia, sinking two ships and killing 300 Union sailors. Union soldiers on the shore and Union ship cannons fired at the *Virginia* but nothing affected the mighty ironclad. An urgent message was sent from President Lincoln to warn northern cities along the coast. When night fell, the *Virginia* pulled close to the southern shore, determined to finish off the rest of the fleet the next day.

John Ericsson, Designer of the Monitor

John Ericsson was born in Sweden in 1803 and was a skilled inventor. He invented the **screw propeller**, which changed the way ships navigated at sea. He also invented a steam engine, rotating turret, and even a deep-sea sounding device.

John Ericsson

Ericsson moved to the United States to work for the U.S. Navy, and in 1844 designed the USS *Princeton*, a modern warship propelled by a screw propeller. Unfortunately, when the guns of the ship exploded in front of government naval officials, the secretaries of state and navy were killed. It wasn't Ericsson's fault, but he retired from working for the navy for a long time after that. He was called back into service during the Civil War, and convinced Abraham Lincoln that his odd design for the *Monitor* would be effective against the Confederacy's ironclad ship. He was right, and the rest is history.

But when the *Virginia* pulled out into open water the next morning, the *Monitor* blocked its way. The *Virginia* opened fire on the *Monitor*, and the fire was returned. The two ships pounded each other for more than four hours, with neither winning. Then, with its crew in a state of confusion after the wounding of their captain, the *Monitor* pulled away. The *Virginia* then pulled away, too, assuming that the *Monitor* had given up.

While neither ship actually won the battle, the success of both ships under the assault of so many cannonballs immediately made every wooden warship **obsolete**. From that point on, the seas were ruled by ironclad ships.

KNOW YOUR CIVIL WAR SLANG

top rail—first class, the best.

WORDS 2 KNOW

screw propeller: a rod with blades that is turned by an engine to move an airplane or ship.

obsolete: no longer made or used.

IRONCLAD SHIPS:
THE *MONITOR* OR THE *VIRGINIA*

IRONCLAD SHIP BASE

SUPPLIES

1 Cut the milk carton in half, lengthwise. This will be the bottom of the ship. Take the other half of the carton and cut off the sides, leaving the flat part for a deck that will cover the entire open space of the hull.

2 Staple the peak of the carton (where the spout was) and duct tape over the staples so it is firmly sealed.

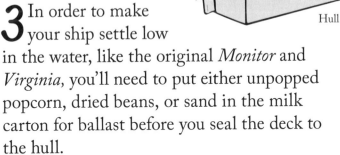

Deck

Staple here

Hull

3 In order to make your ship settle low in the water, like the original *Monitor* and *Virginia*, you'll need to put either unpopped popcorn, dried beans, or sand in the milk carton for ballast before you seal the deck to the hull.

4 Duct tape the deck onto the hull, then cover the hull in duct tape. This is your "iron" cladding.

5 The base for your ironclad ship is now complete and you're ready to make it into the *Monitor* or the *Virginia*!

FOR EACH SHIP:
- **milk carton,** 2 liter or ½ gallon
- **scissors**
- **stapler**
- **duct tape**
- **1–3 cups unpopped popcorn,** dried beans, or sand (for ballast)
- **aluminum foil**

FOR THE *MONITOR*:
- **2 empty tuna cans** or cat food cans, one slightly larger than the other

FOR THE *VIRGINIA*:
- **additional milk carton**
- **empty toilet paper tube**

CONTINUES ON NEXT PAGE . . .

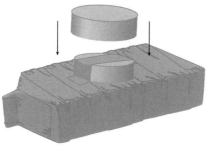 

THE MONITOR

1 Tape the smaller can on the deck, with the opening face down. This will serve as the base for the Monitor's revolving cannon turret. Then place the larger can over the smaller one so that it can rotate around it.

2 Cover the larger can with duct tape, but make sure the can still rotates. If the top can is much bigger than the bottom one, you can crumple tinfoil and stick it around the smaller can. This will allow the turret to turn around the bottom can but still fit snugly.

∾ CIVIL WAR FACTS & TRIVIA ∾

★ Both the *Virginia* and the *Monitor* were destroyed within a year of their historic battle. The Confederate navy destroyed the *Virginia* when the Union took over Norfolk, Virginia, in May 1862. The *Monitor* was being towed from Virginia to North Carolina to help the Union navy when it was caught in a storm and sank.

★ John Ericsson designed every aspect of the *Monitor*, including the first flushing toilets on a ship.

★ The cannons on the *Monitor* fired solid iron cannonballs that weighed 180 pounds each (82 kilograms).

★ Both the North and South built several more ironclad ships during the course of the war, including the Confederate ship *Manassas*, which looked kind of like a giant egg with a cannon sticking out.

THE VIRGINIA

1 Cut both ends off the second milk carton, then cut along the length of one side. You'll have four long panels to work with. Cut off two of the long panels and put them aside. You'll need them later.

2 The other 2-sided panel will be the "barn roof" deckhouse that contained the *Virginia's* mighty cannons. Crease the sides of the outer panels so the deckhouse sits securely on top of the hull (see diagrams to right). Before you tape it to the hull, cut out four small rectangles on each side, where the cannon ports on the original *Virginia* would be.

3 Tape the deckhouse to the hull. Now take the remaining panels from the milk carton and cut two pieces that can fit over the holes in the front and back of the deckhouse. It doesn't matter if they don't fit exactly. Duct tape the entire deckhouse so that it appears ironclad.

4 Finally, create a smokestack by cutting a toilet paper tube about 2 inches long (5 centimeters). Cover it with foil. Tape this onto the top of the deckhouse. Now put both the *Monitor* and *Virginia* into the tub and relive the battle of the ironclads.

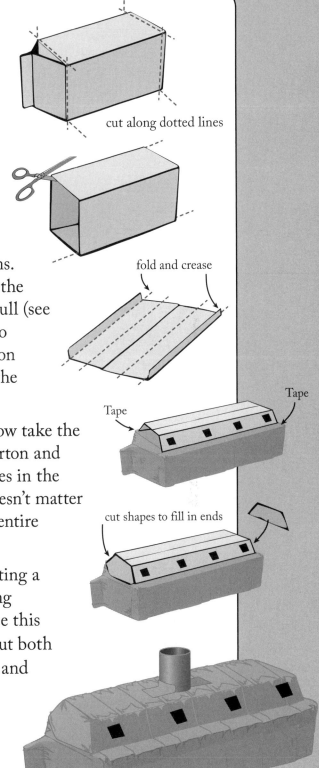

cut along dotted lines

fold and crease

Tape

Tape

cut shapes to fill in ends

ON THE BATTLEFIELD

LEAN-TO SHELTER

S oldiers in both the Union and Confederate armies spent weeks, sometimes months, in the field, marching from one location to the next. A soldier carried a small tent as part of his supplies. In the Confederate army, most soldiers below the rank of staff officer didn't have tents at all. But those who did discovered how hard it was to lug a tent from place to place, and how quickly canvas fell apart and needed repair.

Officers of the One Hundred and Fourteenth Pennsylvania Infantry playing cards in front of tents, Petersburg, Virginia, August 1864.

Every soldier learned how to build a simple lean-to shelter. Usually fallen logs or large branches from trees were available, and when the soldiers were told to set up camp, they scrambled to create a lean-to.

Dog Tents

Old photographs of Civil War camps often show tent cities, where the ground is covered in A-frame tents in rows that stretch as far as you can see. While this was common for the Union army, it wasn't so for the Confederacy. Most Confederate soldiers were lucky if they had a "shelter half" that they could pair with another soldier's shelter half to make what was known as "dog tents," which were two shelter halves buttoned together. Other nicknames for dog tents were dog kennel, picket tent, and pup tent.

Soldiers took two strong branches about 3 or 4 feet in length (about 1 meter), and stuck them into the ground. Another log or heavy branch was tied to the tops of the branches. When a few more branches were leaned against the top branch, the soldiers had the framework for their shelter. They might stretch an extra blanket across the shelter to make a roof. If they did not want to give up their extra blanket, or did not have one, they used moss, leaves, brush, ferns, or whatever was available.

KNOW YOUR CIVIL WAR SLANG

snug as a bug—very comfortable or cozy.

CIVIL WAR FACTS & TRIVIA

★ Soldiers who camped out knew they should make their shelters or set up their tents at least 50 yards away from any body of water, such as a river or a lake. Evaporating water added an extra chill to the air.

★ One of the few times a Confederate soldier lived in a tent was when he first went to training camp.

★ In 1861 the U.S. Army defined the term "bivouac" as "passing the night without shelter, except what could be made with plants and branches."

LEAN-TO SHELTER

1 Push the two branches with the Y at the ends into the ground. It will be easier if you find a part of your lawn that is fairly soft. Make sure you get permission from your parents to build the lean-to in the yard.

2 Now take one of the longer branches and place it across the Y sections. Even though it might be a snug fit, use some of the heavy cord or kite string to tie the branch into place on each end.

SUPPLIES

- **2 strong branches** between 3 and 4 feet in length (about 1 meter), with a Y at one end of each
- **6 branches** between 4 and 5 feet in length (1 to 1½ meters)
- **heavy cord** or kite string
- **old blanket** or large towel

3 Now take the remaining branches and lay them against the top branch at an angle. Carefully nudge the ends into the dirt. This will help keep the branches from falling down or blowing off in the wind. Note that the longer the branches are, the more room you will have in your lean-to shelter! Drape the blanket or towel over the branches.

4 Sit inside your lean-to shelter and try to imagine what life was like for the Civil War soldiers. It's also fun to sleep out in your shelter.

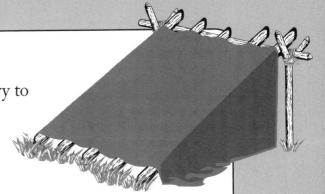

VARIATIONS TO THE OUTDOOR LEAN-TO

If you don't have access to a backyard full of branches, you can use any sort of stick or pole such as broom or rake handles, ski poles, or garden stakes. You could build your lean-to up against the wall of a building. If you decide to do this, you may want some other stabilizing sticks in order to hold it up. If you want to build your lean-to inside, build it against a bed, couch, or other object that is a good height. In both of these cases, use rope or other material to stabilize the lean-to so it won't fall on top of you.

Shelters of All Kinds

Most Union soldiers were issued shelter halves, which were, literally, half a shelter. Shelter halves were pieces of canvas cloth with buttons. Two halves of the shelter could be buttoned together to make a complete tent. Sometimes, three or four soldiers would button their shelter halves together to create a larger tent structure.

A-frame tents, also known as wedge tents, were also used during the first year or so of the Civil War. These were heavy and bulky and had to be carried by wagon. A-frame tents were discontinued early in the war, since they were just too impractical for field use.

Most of the fighting stopped during the winter months. Soldiers built log huts about 5 feet tall (2 meters), using their tents as roofs. They would build fireplaces on one end of the log hut, using sticks or bricks, with a barrel for a chimney.

STEAMBOATS & HOSPITAL SHIPS

*I*n 1807, Robert Fulton designed the first working **steamboat**. For the first time, people were able to travel up and down America's rivers under motorized power, rather than relying on muscle, the **current**, or the wind. Steamboats became the fastest way to transport people and goods up and down United States rivers.

When the Civil War began, control of the country's rivers became more important than ever. Both the Confederate and Union armies had **flotillas** of boats they used as floating **barracks**, supply ships, and gunboats. One floating supply ship was *Red Rover*.

WORDS 2 KNOW

steamboat: a boat with a paddle wheel that is turned by a steam engine. The steam generates power to run the engine.

current: the steady flow of water in one direction.

flotilla: a group or fleet of ships.

barrack: housing for soldiers.

The Confederate steamboat *Red Rover* was on the Mississippi River near St. Louis when it was captured by a Union gunboat. The Confederates tried to sink *Red Rover* to put it out of use, but the Union was able to pull it up and repair it.

*Although the Union needed more gunboats to patrol the Mississippi River, it decided to turn the **Red Rover** into a floating hospital.*

Transporting wounded soldiers by boat was nothing new for either army, but it was usually a terrible experience for soldiers who were already in bad shape. The boats were loud, dirty, and rarely had the supplies or staff necessary to treat illness or injury. Transport ships usually picked up wounded soldiers at the port closest to the battle and dropped them off at the nearest friendly hospital.

KNOW YOUR CIVIL WAR SLANG

sawbones—a surgeon.

Red Rover, *the navy's first hospital ship, built in 1859.*

Contrabands to Freedom

For many runaway slaves in the South, the best chance for freedom was to get on board a Union boat like *Red Rover* as it steamed up or down the Mississippi River. Contraband is illegal trade, which is moving something from one place to another when it is against the law. These runaway slaves were called "contraband." Many ships hired them to serve as cabin boys, carpenters, laborers, cooks, stewards, crewman, and nurses. Working on board *Red Rover* had many advantages, including the pay. The ship's records show that several chambermaids were paid $20 a month for their work. In comparison, the base pay for men in the infantry in the Union army was only $13 a month.

WORDS 2 KNOW

innovation: a new idea or invention.

draft: the depth of water needed to float a ship.

Red Rover was refitted with **innovations** never before found on a ship, all designed to help the sick and wounded. It had separate operating and amputation rooms, and the windows were covered with gauze to keep cinders and smoke from the smokestacks away from the patients.

Rooms at the back of the ship had open walls to allow for better air circulation. Patients who had contagious diseases, such as measles and typhus, were put in these back rooms, as well as on several separate floating barges attached to the back of the ship. This helped keep contagious diseases from infecting everyone on board.

Red Rover also carried enough medical and food supplies for 200 patients and the entire crew for up to three months. Everything the hospital staff needed was on board.

Medical supply boat Planter *at General Hospital wharf on the Appomattox River.*

Steamboats

One reason for the success of steamboats during the 1800s was that they were perfect for river travel. Most had a **draft** of less than 6 or 7 feet (2 meters), which meant they were able to steam up and down the wide, shallow rivers of the American West much better than any deep-hulled boats. The problem with them, however, was that their flat hulls were very difficult to maneuver if the weather or water got rough, since steering a steamboat was very much like steering a giant box.

Red Rover's reputation as a hospital with comfortable accommodations and a caring medical staff grew quickly. In fact, fleet commander Charles Henry Davis had to issue an order limiting the number of patients being sent to the ship—it seemed like every sick or injured soldier wanted to be cared for on *Red Rover*.

Acting Assistant Surgeon George Hopkins from the USS Red Rover.

In addition to being the first complete floating hospital, **Red Rover's** *crew included the first women serving in the U.S. armed forces, as well as the first African-American women hired by either side.*

Red Rover's hospital duties came to an end after the Battle of Vicksburg in 1863, when the Union took control of most of the rivers. For the rest of the war, *Red Rover* was again used to transport supplies.

∽ CIVIL WAR FACTS & TRIVIA ∾

★ The women who served as nurses on *Red Rover* are credited with being the first women to serve on board a naval vessel. In most accounts, the nuns who served on *Red Rover* are recognized as the first U.S. naval nurses, even though the ship's records show that runaway slave women were hired after being welcomed on board, making them the first paid female naval employees.

★ From the end of the Civil War to 1908, women were not allowed to serve in the navy.

★ The majority of *Red Rover's* crew was African-American. At one point, there were twice as many black sailors and crew as white.

STEAMBOAT

1 Cut the large milk container in half lengthwise. Staple the spout together and tape over it—if it isn't watertight your boat will sink. This will serve as the hull of your boat. Use any color duct tape to cover up the graphics on the carton. Keep the rest of the carton to use for other pieces later.

2 Take the small milk carton and cut off the sides of the spout. Tape over the remaining side so you create a rectangular box. This will be your pilot house. If you want to decorate it to look like an old-fashioned steamboat like *Red Rover*, cover the pilot house in white paper and draw or cut out windows. Tape this to the floor of the hull.

3 Decorate the toilet paper tubes to look like smokestacks with white on the bottom and a black rim around the top. Tape the toilet paper tubes on each end of the pilot house.

4 To make the paddle, tape one popsicle stick to each side of the hull, making sure half of each stick juts out beyond the back of the boat.

SUPPLIES

- **milk carton**, half gallon or 2 liter
- **scissors**
- **stapler**
- **duct tape**
- **milk carton**, quart or liter
- **white and black paper**
- **2 toilet paper tubes**
- **markers or paint**
- **2 popsicle or craft sticks**
- **cork**
- **Xacto knife**
- **1 rubber band**
- **unpopped popcorn, dried beans, or sand** for ballast

★ ★ ★ 44 ★ ★ ★

5 Have an adult help with this step. Take the cork and use the Xacto knife to make four slits along the length of the cork, equal distances apart.

6 Cut two paddle blades from a leftover piece of milk carton. The blades will need to be the same length as the cork and wide enough to catch water. Make sure they aren't so wide that they will hit the back of your boat when you attach the paddlewheel to the sticks.

7 Slide the blades into two opposite slits on the cork. Slide the rubber band firmly into the other slits as shown above and then stretch the rubber band around the outside of the popsicle sticks.

8 From the remaining half of the milk carton, cut out two half-circles that are the same length as the popsicle sticks. Decorate the plain side of these with the name of your ship. Tape these over the popsicle sticks with the flat side facing the water. Make sure you can still wind the cork paddlewheel and that the paddlewheel moves freely.

9 Place your ship in the water, wind up the paddlewheel, and let her go. You may find that the boat is easier to maneuver with a little weight, or ballast, in the bottom of the hull.

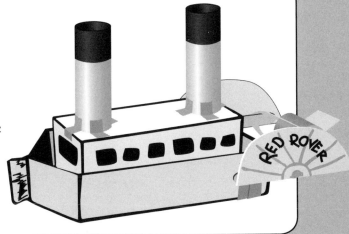

*O*ne of the biggest innovations of the Civil War was the change in how war was waged. Weapons in past wars had been so inaccurate and slow to reload that most of the fighting was at close range. Armies marched toward each other in formation, then each set up two lines of fighters. The first line knelt to shoot and the second line stood and shot over the front line.

KNOW YOUR CIVIL WAR SLANG

possum—a buddy.

picket—a guard or guard duty.

Soldiers discovered that weapons had changed during the Civil War. The Gatling gun fired 250 rounds a minute from six barrels. Repeating rifles, breech-loading cannons, and other weapons were not only more accurate, they shot farther and were much easier and faster to reload.

These weapons were so different from what had been used earlier that, in the four years that the Civil War was waged, the entire theory of how to fight a war changed.

At the beginning of the war, soldiers massed together and charged the enemy, ready for close, hand-to-hand fighting. Battles ended quickly with decisive victories. Ulysses S. Grant said about earlier wars that, "A man might fire at you all day without you finding it out." Now soldiers found that charging toward an enemy whose guns could reload quickly and shoot from half a mile away meant that men were killed and injured in shocking numbers.

The first Union wagons moving into Petersburg.

Later in the war, the Union and Confederate armies were stuck in battles that could last for months at a time. Armies dug trenches and stayed in them. They didn't actively fight very often. This was siege warfare—waiting out their enemy. The Siege of Petersburg, Virginia, took 10 months. Lots of soldiers, especially southern soldiers defending the city, dug and then lived in trenches.

Trench system and soldiers in the trenches. Petersburg, Virginia, 1865.

This style of fighting called for new ways of keeping track of the enemy. Soldiers needed to see what their enemies were doing while they sat in their trenches, without having to pop up and maybe get shot. The best tool for this was the **periscope**.

Thomas Doughty, a naval officer for the Union, is given credit for inventing the periscope for his gunship, the USS *Osage*. Gunners on the ship couldn't see the high banks of Louisiana's Red River out of the peepholes of the ship, so Doughty used his periscope to see above the turret and direct his guns.

WORDS 2 KNOW

periscope: a tube with a set of mirrors for viewing objects or people that are out of sight.

casualty: someone killed or injured in battle.

The periscope quickly became a useful tool for soldiers in the trenches. It helped them to see what was going on outside the trenches, without being harmed in the process.

∿ CIVIL WAR FACTS & TRIVIA ∿

★ During the Siege of Petersburg, soldiers dug trenches about 3 feet deep and 6 to 8 feet wide (1 meter deep and 2–3 meters wide). In front of these trenches were small rifle pits, which were large enough for two riflemen. Trenches were sometimes big enough to hold wagons.

★ During long battles or sieges, soldiers would sleep in small shelters built of earth and sandbags, or in caves dug in the trenches. These shelters were usually very small and uncomfortable, but were bulletproof and protected soldiers overnight.

★ The trench lines dug during the Siege of Petersburg ran for 53 miles (85 kilometers). By the end of the siege, there had been 61,000 Union **casualties** and 38,000 Confederate casualties.

PERISCOPE

1 Have an adult help you cut off the top of one milk carton, removing the spout. Cut a hole near the bottom of one side of the milk carton (see diagram). Make sure to leave about ¼ inch of carton around the hole (just over ½ centimeter.)

2 Turn the milk carton on its side, with the hole facing you. On the side facing up, measure 2¾ inches up from the bottom of the carton (7 centimeters) and draw a diagonal line from the bottom corner closest to you to the mark you made.

3 Have an adult help you use the Xacto knife. Cut a slit on that line, but don't cut all the way to the edge of the carton. This is where you will place your mirror, and it works best if the mirror fits in the slot snugly.

4 Slide your mirror into the cut so that the mirror faces the hole in the carton. Hold it up and look through the hole at the mirror. You should be able to see out the top of the milk carton. If you can't, adjust the mirror so that you have a clear view out of the top of the milk carton. Tape the mirror loosely in place.

SUPPLIES

- **2 quart-size milk or juice cartons** (1 liter)
- **Xacto knife**
- **ruler**
- **pen**
- **2 small hand mirrors** (flat, pocket-sized ones are best)
- **tape**

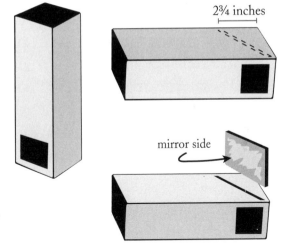

2¾ inches

mirror side

CONTINUES ON NEXT PAGE . . .

5 Repeat steps 1–4 with the other milk carton.

6 Stand one carton on the table, with the hole facing you. Put the other carton on the table upside down, with the mirror on the top and the hole facing away from you.

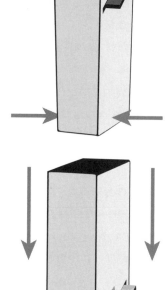

7 Put the carton with the hole facing away from you on top of the one with the hole facing you. You should be able to squeeze the top carton slightly to fit it into the bottom one. Tape these together.

8 Look through the bottom hole. You should be able to see out of the top milk carton, which will be about a foot higher than your normal field of vision. Imagine you are in a trench with bullets whizzing over your head. Sticking a periscope up would be a lot safer than sticking your head out. Try looking around corners or over the back of a sofa using your periscope.

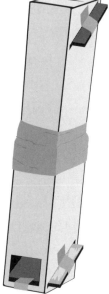

KNOW YOUR CIVIL WAR SLANG

· ·

bombproof—an underground shelter. Also an officer or soldier who never fought in battles.

· ·

hornets—bullets.

SOLDIERS' FOOD

During the war, each soldier was given the same amount of food each week or month, called rations. These rations included a cracker-like biscuit called hardtack, dried or salted beef or pork, coffee, and dried fruits and vegetables. They also received flour or cornmeal as well as sugar, beans, tea, salt, and potatoes.

Hardtack, also known as sheet iron crackers.

It was simple food, often lacking in certain required nutrients, such as vitamin C. This resulted in a disease called scurvy, which could cause death. Sutlers traveled to army camps to sell foods that weren't issued to soldiers through rations, such as milk or fresh vegetables. This food was often too expensive for soldiers, so they settled for what they had. Sometimes soldiers wrote home requesting that a certain food or drink be sent to them, but this only worked if a soldier was going to be at camp for an extended period of time.

Officers dining out.

KNOW YOUR CIVIL WAR SLANG

vittles—food or rations.

bread basket—stomach.

grab a root—have a potato for dinner.

mess—cooking and eating food together.

messmates—soldiers who cooked and ate together.

Food rations were uncooked, so the soldiers had to prepare their own meals. This meant they had to start a fire and find water if it wasn't given to them, which was often difficult.

Both the Confederate and Union armies had Commissary Departments to organize food distribution. The Commissary Department was responsible for purchasing the food, transporting it to the troops, and keeping the food from going bad in the process. Sometimes a herd of cattle would move with the army, providing fresh meat. But most of the time meat was smoked or salted to keep it from spoiling, and fruits and vegetables were dried.

Hardtack kept well unless it got wet: then mold and bugs made hardtack their home. Soldiers dropped the hardtack into a hot cup of coffee, killing the bugs. When the bugs floated to the top, they could skim them off the surface, and be left with coffee and softened bread.

Commissary depot with supply train wagons, Cedar Level, Virginia.

Soldiers in both the North and the South suffered from food shortages. They often marched to new locations faster than their supplies could keep up. In many cases, the armies just couldn't provide enough food for all of the men fighting. Soldiers on both sides **foraged** for food in the countryside, taking livestock and crops. This often meant stealing from **civilians**. It became such a problem that foraging was outlawed and soldiers caught were arrested.

WORDS 2 KNOW

forage: to search for food or provisions, and live off the land.

civilian: a person who is not a soldier.

malnourishment: poorly fed or not fed enough.

CIVIL WAR FACTS & TRIVIA

★ One of the most popular dishes for soldiers (when they could get it) was baked beans. It was so popular that three songs about baked beans were written during the war. Robert E. Lee is reported to have said about his troops, "All I would have to do to keep them happy is to give them beans three times every day."

★ Coffee was considered the most important food for northern armies, while tobacco was treasured by southern armies. On rare occasions, Union and Confederate soldiers met on picket lines and traded these items with one another.

★ Before the Civil War began, a southern family spent about $6–7 per month on food. This included the basics, as well as anything they didn't grow themselves. By 1864, however, groceries cost that same family about $400 per month. The scarcity and expense of food caused **malnourishment** in many families.

★ If soldiers were lucky, they received meat, vegetables, and condensed milk vacuum-packed in tin cans or jars. These packaging processes had just been invented and allowed food to stay "fresh" over long periods of time.

SOLDIER VITTLES

UNION HARDTACK

1 Preheat oven to 350 degrees Fahrenheit (177 degrees Celsius). Mix all ingredients together. Make sure you add enough flour so that the dough is no longer sticky, but be careful not to make it too dry. Knead the dough a few times. It is easiest to roll the dough directly on an ungreased cookie sheet. Bake for about 30 minutes.

2 Remove the sheet from the oven and cut the large square into smaller 3-by-3-inch squares (7½ by 7½ centimeters). Poke 16 evenly spaced holes in each square. Flip, return to the oven, and bake for another 30 minutes. Turn the oven off, and allow the hardtack to cool in the oven with the door closed. Allow to completely cool, and then enjoy!

SUPPLIES

- **2 cups flour** (260 grams)
- **½ to ¾ cup water** (120 to 180 milliliters)
- **salt** (5–6 pinches)
- **bowl and spoon**
- **rolling pin**
- **cookie sheet**
- **knife**

CONFEDERATE JOHNNY CAKES

1 Preheat oven to 350 degrees Fahrenheit (177 degrees Celsius). Mix all ingredients until the batter is quite stiff. Form about eight biscuits and place them on a lightly greased cookie sheet.

2 Bake for about 20 minutes or until light brown. Allow to cool. Spread with butter or molasses, or eat it plain like the Confederates did.

SUPPLIES

- **2 cups cornmeal** (260 grams)
- **⅔ cup milk** (158 milliliters)
- **2 tablespoons vegetable oil** (30 grams)
- **2 teaspoons baking soda** (10 grams)
- **½ teaspoon salt** (2½ grams)
- **bowl and spoon**
- **cookie sheet**
- **butter or molasses**

TELEGRAPHS & MORSE CODE

Many historians consider the Civil War the first modern war. This was because of innovations in weapons and battle tactics, as well as because of advances in communication. Samuel Morse was a New York inventor and successful painter. In 1844 he perfected a way to send coded messages from one location to another using electric pulses sent through wires, creating the first reliable telegraph.

Samuel Morse

Teams constructing telegraph lines, April 1864.

Morse also invented a code to send messages along the wires. Known as Morse code, it uses a series of dots and dashes to create words. Telegraph operators translated the dots and dashes into English words.

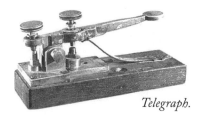

Telegraph.

Congress gave Samuel Morse $30,000 to create a telegraph system running from Washington, D.C., to Baltimore, Maryland. The fastest and cheapest way to build it was to string the lines on trees and poles from Baltimore to Washington. That's how poles and wires became part of the American landscape.

Telegraph battery wagon.

The first electronic message to travel these lines was sent on May 24, 1844. Morse transmitted the words "what God hath wrought" from the office of the Supreme Court in Washington, D.C., to a train station in Baltimore, Maryland. The telegraph would forever change communication. By 1861, telegraph lines ran from coast to coast.

The best way to learn Morse code is to memorize the sounds each letter makes. Dots sound like "dit." Dashes sound like "dah." The letters "SOS," the famous plea to "save our ship," sounds like this: "dit dit dit, dah dah dah, dit dit dit."

Who Were They?

About 2,000 people were employed as telegraph workers in the year before the start of the Civil War. Most were men, but as many as 200 women also worked as telegraphers. One of the first women telegraphers was Sarah G. Bagley, a known women's rights **activist** and newspaper editor. She helped make telegraphy the first technical career open to women.

The telegraph became important for communication during the war, and military telegraphers were vital in relaying important military information. These workers were both men and women. Despite their important contribution to the war effort, the living and working conditions for military telegraphers were miserable. They did not receive pay or **pension** as normal soldiers did, and they often were placed in highly dangerous zones without adequate protection. Many of them died of disease or injury during the war.

WORDS 2 KNOW

activist: a person who fights for something they believe in.

pension: a regular payment made by the government after service ends.

Field telegraph station in Virginia.

KNOW YOUR CIVIL WAR SLANG

. . . .

jawings—talking.

. . . .

picket line—the line between Confederate and Union soldiers on the battlefield.

Transmitting messages via telegraph became a standard method of communication.

The telegraph also had a huge impact on how the Civil War was fought and won. In the Revolutionary War and the War of 1812, armies relied on messages delivered on foot or by horseback. As a result, changes in battle strategy were very slow. In the Civil War, both sides used telegraph teams to relay information from one place to another in a matter of minutes. For the first time, armies were able to communicate with each other over long distances very quickly. This meant that they could make important battlefield decisions immediately.

∽ CIVIL WAR FACTS & TRIVIA ∽

★ The telegraph was an important tool for communication on the battlefield, but it was also an important tool for spies. Both sides intercepted telegraphed messages in order to learn each others' battle plans.

★ More than 15,000 miles of telegraph lines were strung for use by both Union and Confederate armies during the Civil War.

★ The Telegraph Service wasn't part of either the Union or Confederate army, and the telegraph operators were civilians. More than 300 telegraph operators died during the Civil War, and their families received no pension or other support from the government.

★ President Lincoln did not have immediate access to telegraph wires, as they didn't go directly to the White House. He had to cross the street to a telegraph office to check messages.

Civil War Balloons

Did you know that both the Union and Confederate armies conducted aerial **reconnaissance**? They tried to spy on each other's armies from the air. How did it work? By balloon!

The most famous balloonist from the Civil War was Thaddeus Lowe. Lowe realized that hot air balloons would be perfect vehicles for spying on the Confederates. He convinced President Lincoln to establish a Balloon Corps and built the first Union balloon. Named *The Union*, this balloon went up 1,000 feet (300 meters) over Washington, D.C., still tied to the ground. Lowe spied on Confederate troops more than 3 miles away (5 kilometers), and telegraphed information to the troops below. Union troops were able to fire on the Confederates without even seeing where they were from the ground. This was such a successful mission that Lowe was given the money to build six more balloons for the Balloon Corps.

reconnaissance: military observation to locate an enemy.

The Confederate army also had a small balloon corps, led by Captain John Bryan. The Confederates built two balloons. One was used for about a year over the skies of Richmond before it escaped in high wind and was captured by the Union. The other one never even made it into the sky.

Balloons gave both the Union and Confederate armies information about each other that they couldn't have received any other way. But it turned out that balloon reconnaissance was too risky and too expensive. The Union Balloon Corps was disbanded in 1863.

Thaddeus Lowe observing the battle from his balloon Intrepid, *Fair Oaks, Virginia.*

TELEGRAPH

1 To make the key, take one of the pieces of wood and screw down one end of one of the 4-inch-long pieces of metal strapping. Screw another wood screw directly into the wood at the other end of the block so the bent strapping (as shown) will make a connection with the screw if you push down on it. This will be your telegraph key. The key should not touch the screw unless you push down on it.

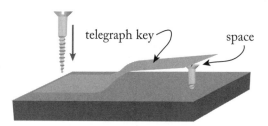

telegraph key   space

2 To make the battery holder, measure the length of the two batteries placed end to end, and mark the length on the second piece of wood. Screw two of the 4-inch strips of strapping to the wood at either end of the mark so the strapping will touch the connections on the bottoms, or "ends," of the batteries.

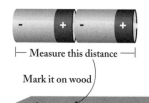

⊢ Measure this distance ⊣

Mark it on wood

SUPPLIES

- **2 pieces of wood,** each 4–6 inches long and 2–3 inches wide (10–15 centimeters long and 5–7½ centimeters wide)
- **9 small wood screws or nails**
- **screwdriver and hammer**
- **3 flat strips of metal strapping** from the hardware store, about 4 inches long (10 centimeters); NOTE: metal strapping must be iron-bearing or "ferrous" metal (metal that is attracted by a magnet)
- **1 flat strip of metal strapping** about 7 inches long (18 centimeters)
- **ruler**
- **2 C or 2 D batteries**
- **large rubber band**
- **2 large iron nails** 2–3 inches long (5–7½ centimeters)
- **20 feet or more of insulated solid wire** (6 meters) about ¹⁄₆₄ inch or less in diameter (0.4 millimeters) from the hardware store
- **wire cutters**

3 Place the batteries in the holder, and put the rubber band around the metal strapping to keep it pressed against the battery contacts.

4 To make the sounder, nail one of the long iron nails into the piece of wood with the battery holder. Attach one end of the insulated wire to the closer screw on the battery holder. Wind about 100 turns of the insulated wire around the nail, and attach the other end of the wire to the screw under the telegraph key on the other piece of wood.

5 Take the 7-inch-long piece of metal strapping and screw it to the piece of wood so that you can bend it up and over the long nail with the insulated wire wound around it. When the battery is connected, the electric current will pass through the wire, making the nail into an electromagnet. It will pull the piece of bent metal down onto it, making a clicking sound. Make sure the metal is bent close enough to the nail so it will connect when the battery is connected.

6 Take the second iron nail and hammer it in right next to the metal strapping, close to the nail with the wire wrapped around it, so the metal strapping is tucked just under the head of the nail. This nail will keep the metal strapping from pulling too far from the electromagnet. It also makes a clicking sound when the metal strapping is released by the magnet and moves upward.

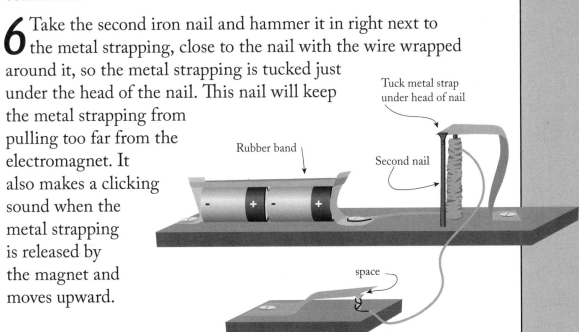

Tuck metal strap under head of nail

Rubber band

Second nail

space

CONTINUES ON NEXT PAGE . . .

7 Cut another small piece of wire and attach it to the other screw holding down the key. Take the other end of this wire and attach it to the screw holding the other side of the battery holder onto the wood.

8 When you push down on the telegraph key so it touches the screw, you complete the circuit. This allows electricity to flow from the batteries through the sounder's coil. As the metal strip hits the nail in the center of the coil it makes a clicking sound. When you release the key, it breaks the circuit and the metal strip hits the other nail, making a different clicking noise. These two sounds form the dots and dashes of Morse code.

9 Using the Morse code chart shown here, try tapping out your own Civil War telegraph message.

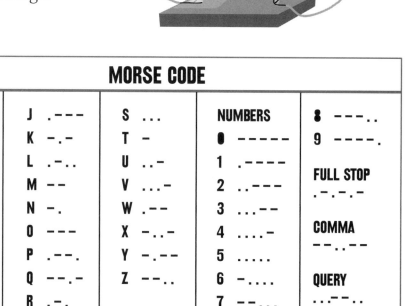

Sound from here

Push down here

space

MORSE CODE

A .−	J .−−−	S ...	**NUMBERS**	8 −−−..
B −−...	K −.−	T −	0 −−−−−	9 −−−−.
C −.−.	L .−..	U ..−	1 .−−−−	
D −..	M −−	V ...−	2 ..−−−	**FULL STOP**
E .	N −.	W .−−	3 ...−−	.−.−.−
F ..−.	O −−−	X −..−	4 ....−	
G −−.	P .−−.	Y −.−−	5	**COMMA**
H	Q −−.−	Z −−..	6 −....	−−..−−
I ..	R .−.		7 −−...	**QUERY** ..−−..

SIGNAL FLAGS

*I*n addition to communicating by telegraph, both armies in the Civil War communicated by signal flags in a system known as wig-wag. The signal system was developed in the 1850s by an army doctor named Albert Myer.

The wig-wag system was designed so soldiers could communicate visual signals to each other over long distances, up to a few miles away. Soldiers used one of three flags: a white flag with a red square, a red flag with a white square, or a black flag with a white square. If the soldier was signaling from a hill or at sea, a red flag would be more easily seen. From a wooded area, a white flag would show up better, and if it was snowy, a black flag would be most visible. At night, signalmen replaced their flags with torches.

Signal station on the Ogeechee River at Fort McAllister, Georgia.

Signaling in wig-wag could be very dangerous work. The signalmen had to be high up so that the signals could be seen from a distance. Usually the signal station was at the highest point closest to the battle area. When there were no hills or naturally high places, troops built towers for signal stations. This made members of the signal corps especially visible targets for the enemy.

Signal Corps, Central Signal Station, Washington, D.C.

Signal Flag Stars

While most signal flags had a square in the middle, some Signal Corps officers were awarded a signal flag with a red star in the center. These were special flags given to officers who had done a great job in combat. The points of the star sometimes had the names of specific battles written on them where the Signal Corps unit had been most effective in battle.

THE WIG-WAG CODE

Each letter of the wig-wag alphabet was represented by a certain position or movement of the flag. Messages were spelled out according to a letter–number code. Each letter of the alphabet was represented by a combination of numbers, and the numbers corresponded to flag movement.

A movement to the left of the center meant a "1," and a movement to the right of center meant a "2." The letter A, for example, was "11," which is two movements from the left to the center. Dipping the flag forward one or more times signaled the end of a word, sentence, or message.

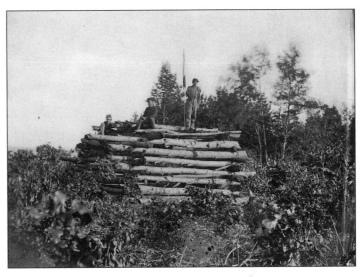

Signal tower overlooking Antietam Battlefield, Elk Mountain, Maryland.

Both Confederate and Union Signal Corps units were skilled at sending messages via wig-wag. Each side developed its own wig-wag code so the other side couldn't understand the messages being relayed. Both the Union and Confederate Signal Corps spent lots of time and energy inventing new codes and trying to break each other's codes.

∽ CIVIL WAR FACTS & TRIVIA ∽

★ In the Union army, only officers were trusted with the signal code. They would call out the number combinations to Signal Corps sergeants, who would actually move the flag. Many sergeants learned the code through continued use. The Confederates, on the other hand, taught all of their Signal Corps personnel the code.

★ The Confederates first used the wig-wag signaling system in combat during the First Battle of Bull Run. A signalman on a hilltop saw the shine of bayonets and signaled to his fellow soldiers, "Look out for your left; you are turned." His signal helped the Confederates win the battle.

Civil War Signal Corps

Here are the flag signals that were used by the Signal Corps during the Civil War.

Ready

1

2

3

4

5

Here is the alphabet using these number signals.

A	B	C	D	E	F	G	H	I	J	K	L	M
11	1423	234	111	23	1114	1142	231	2	2231	1434	114	2314

N	O	P	Q	R	S	T	U	V	W	X	Y	Z
22	14	2343	2342	142	143	1	223	2311	2234	1431	222	1111

5—the end of a word.

55—the end of a sentence.

555—the end of a message.

ON THE BATTLEFIELD
UNIFORMS

*U*niforms in the Civil War were as varied as the people who wore them. When the Civil War began in 1861, no one expected it to last for more than a few months. The Union army had only 16,000 soldiers, and the Confederates had no army at all at first. Because neither the North nor the South was prepared for war, the problem of uniforms came up almost immediately. Recruiting posters in the South made it clear to men who signed up that, "Volunteers shall furnish their own clothes." But providing uniforms to soldiers was a problem for both sides.

WORDS 2 KNOW

standardized: all the same.

militia: people with military training who are called up only during an emergency.

One of the biggest challenges facing both armies was to quickly outfit their troops in **standardized** uniforms. This was necessary to help each side tell themselves apart from the enemy. Most soldiers wore their everyday clothes. But some men who joined to fight wore the uniforms they had from their home state's **militia**, or from earlier wars.

KNOW YOUR CIVIL WAR SLANG

gray backs—southern soldiers.

chicken guts—officer's gold braiding on his cuff.

Southern militias had blue uniforms that looked almost identical to the Union army's blue jackets, and some northern militia units had uniforms that looked nothing like standard Union clothes. So shortly after the war began, both armies set out rules for what its soldiers would wear.

The southern army's official uniform was a short jacket and pants made of something called "jean." This was a rugged blend of cotton and wool, dyed gray or brown. The Union army's standard uniform was a blue wool suit made from shoddy, which was a material made from old and new wool. Infantry soldiers had a long jacket, while cavalry soldiers wore a short jacket. At the beginning of the war, the uniform pants were dark blue, but later in the war the regulation uniform was a dark blue coat with light blue pants.

The forage cap or kepi was the standard issue cap for all enlisted men in the Union army and most of the Confederate army. It had a round, flat top and a visor.

Colors for Different Branches

One way to tell different divisions apart on the battlefield was by the color of the trim on their uniforms. Both Union and Confederate soldiers used the same color coding. Cavalrymen wore yellow trim on their uniforms, dragoons wore orange, mounted riflemen wore emerald green, infantry wore light "French" blue, and artillerymen wore red. Medical personnel wore black trim on their uniforms, while generals, staff, and engineer officers wore buff (cream-colored) trim. Officers wore a stripe sewn down the leg of their pants, and the stripe would be in the color of their division.

Zouave

Zouave comes from an Algerian word, and the original Zouave units were native Algerian and North African fighters who joined the French Foreign Legion. They were known for their fierce fighting style, flashy uniforms, and incredible bravery. Interest in the Zouave fighters was sparked in the United States because of a man named Elmer Ephraim Ellsworth. He learned about Zouave fighters while in Europe, and decided to start his own militia unit devoted to Zouave-style drilling. His Zouave unit toured the country, amazing audiences with their drilling skill and fancy uniforms. Zouaves wore baggy, colorful pants that bloused at the ankle, white gaiters worn over their shoes, a wide sash, a short jacket worn over a plain shirt, and a white turban or fez. The tour sparked a "Zouave fever" in the 1850s. When the war broke out, Zouave units fought in both Confederate and Union armies, although some soldiers changed to traditional uniforms when they realized that their colorful clothes made them a more visible target.

Band of the One Hundred and Fourteenth Pennsylvania Infantry (Zouaves), Brandy Station, Virginia.

Each soldier was also given a belt set that had a cartridge box, a bayonet, and a scabbard—or holder—for his rifle. Soldiers carried a canteen and canvas backpack, and a blanket roll with a half-shelter, wool blanket, and sometimes a rubber blanket or poncho.

Southern soldiers almost never had as much gear as northern soldiers, mostly because there were so many supply shortages in the South. The Union army had an easier time outfitting its troops, since most of the factories were in the North and they could get good-quality material from Europe.

WORDS 2 KNOW

custom-made: made to exactly fit one person.

mass-produce: to make large quantities of things in factories.

Even the Union army had a difficult time getting uniforms to its soldiers because of the amount of time it took to make them. All clothing up to the 1860s was **custom-made** and a single uniform could take as long as 14 hours to finish.

The Union army solved some of its uniform problems by creating **mass-produced** clothing in just a few sizes: small, medium, and large. Most soldiers fit pretty well into one of the standard sizes, and the rest had to make do. This is the first time lots of clothing was made to fit a lot of people pretty well, rather than making less clothing that fit each person perfectly. It became the standard way of manufacturing clothing all over the world after the war.

Officers of Third Pennsylvania Heavy Artillery in their uniforms, Fort Monroe, Virginia.

∾ CIVIL WAR FACTS & TRIVIA ∾

★ Union soldiers nicknamed Confederates "butternuts" because the dye used to make the southern uniforms came from actual butternuts. The color was often uneven and turned a tan-gray color over time.

★ The wool blend material known as "shoddy" used to make the Union uniforms was of poor quality. It fell apart so quickly that the word "shoddy" quickly came to mean "of poor quality" or "poorly made."

KEPI

1 Cut four strips of cardboard about 8 inches long by 2 inches wide (20 centimeters by 5 centimeters). These will form the base of your hat.

2 Staple three of the four cardboard strips together lengthwise. Wrap this strip around your head. If it is too small, add another cardboard strip and measure again. Staple the ends together so that the cardboard ring headband fits snugly on your head, then cut off any extra cardboard.

3 Cut one sheet of felt lengthwise, down the middle. This will give you two 4¼-by-11-inch pieces of felt (10½ by 27½ centimeters). Stick or staple one of the felt strips to the cardboard ring. The long edge of the felt should line up with the bottom edge of the cardboard. Do the same to the second felt strip, so that you have a complete circle of felt. You can cut another piece of felt down the middle and use one of these extra strips if you need it.

4 The top of the kepi is smaller than the headband. Make a circle out of cardboard about 5 inches in diameter (13 centimeters). Make a circle of felt about half an inch wider than the cardboard circle, and glue the two circles together.

SUPPLIES

- **tape measure**
- **scissors**
- **sheet of cardboard** or an old manila file folder
- **stapler**
- **black or gray felt**, sticky-backed if available, 8½-by-11-inch sheets (21 by 27½ centimeters)
- **glue stick**
- **gold or black pipe cleaner** or ribbon

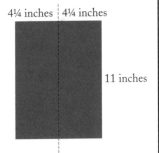

4¼ inches | 4¼ inches

11 inches

felt

cardboard

5 inches

★ ★ ★ 71 ★ ★ ★

CONTINUES ON NEXT PAGE . . .

5 Now lay the circle over the top edge of the hat. Since the top of the hat is smaller than the bottom, make the felt overlap at the top, so it fits the circle (see diagram). Staple or glue the top sides of the hat to keep this shape.

6 Put glue around the outside rim of the circle and lay the hat on the circle. Pull the ends of the circle around the hat so the glue has something to adhere to. Sticky felt will easily stick to the sides of the hat felt.

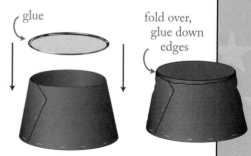

glue

fold over, glue down edges

7 To make the bill of your kepi, measure and cut out the two shapes shown here (to the right) on cardboard. Use the cardboard pieces as templates to cut the shapes out of felt.

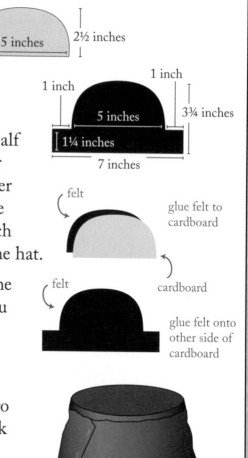

5 inches   2½ inches

1 inch

1 inch

5 inches

3¾ inches

1¼ inches

7 inches

8 Glue the half circle of felt to the half circle of cardboard. Glue the other piece of felt, with the tabs, to the other side of the cardboard. This will be the bottom of your hat bill, and will attach the bill to the cardboard rim inside the hat.

felt

glue felt to cardboard

9 Glue the felt rim of the bill onto the cardboard rim inside the hat. If you are having trouble keeping it on with glue, staple it. Let sit until it's dry.

felt

cardboard

glue felt onto other side of cardboard

10 Finally, cut a piece of ribbon or pipe cleaner long enough to go around the front of your hat. Use black for a Confederate hat, and gold for a Union hat. Glue the ribbon to the seam on the hat, just above the bill.

ZOUAVE FEZ

Fezzes were worn by Zouaves. They are stiff hats that perch on top of the head rather than slouching down like a kepi.

1 Cut four strips of cardboard, each 5 inches long by 4 inches tall (12½ by 10 centimeters).

2 Staple three of the four cardboard strips together lengthwise. Wrap this strip around the top of your head snugly, so that the cardboard strips make a kind of cone shape. If it is too small, add another cardboard strip and measure again.

3 Cut one sheet of felt lengthwise, down the middle. This will give you two, 4½-by-11-inch pieces of felt (10½ by 27½ centimeters). Glue the pieces of felt to the outside of the cardboard, covering it completely. Then refit the fez to your head and staple the ends together so that the cardboard ring fits snugly on your head.

SUPPLIES

- **tape measure**
- **scissors**
- **sheet of cardboard** or old manila file folder
- **stapler**
- **red or black felt,** sticky-backed if available, 8½ by 11 sheets (21 by 27½ centimeters)
- **glue stick**
- **yarn tassel**

KNOW YOUR CIVIL WAR SLANG

Zuzu—Zouaves.

housewife—a sewing kit.

Bummer's cap—regulation fatigue or forage cap.

Bummer—a loafer, a forager, or someone safe in the rear.

CONTINUES ON NEXT PAGE . . .

4 The top of the fez is smaller than the bottom of the headband. Make a circle out of cardboard that's about 4 inches in diameter (10 centimeters). Adjust this if necessary to fit the top of your cardboard ring. Cut a circle of felt about half an inch wider than the cardboard circle, and glue the two circles together.

5 Poke a small hole in the center of the circle, and thread a tassel through the hole. Tie a knot in the end of the yarn on the inside, so when the top of the fez is glued to the sides, the tassel will be on the outside.

6 Now turn the fez over and fit the circle onto the top edge of the felt. Then put glue around the outside rim of the circle and lay the hat on the circle. Pull the ends of the circle around the hat so the glue has something to adhere to. Sticky felt will easily stick to the sides of the hat felt.

Make Like a Zouave

You can make a modified Zouave uniform by wearing baggy sweatpants stuffed into white sports socks, a solid color long-sleeve T-shirt, and a vest. Tie a wide scarf around your waist. You may feel like a clown, but many modern clown costumes—such as some Shriners wear—look similar to the Zouave uniforms worn during the Civil War.

ON THE HOMEFRONT

The unexpected length of the war and level of destruction created serious hardship for those at home. Civilians in the North were affected by the war mostly through shortages of certain goods, and the absence of fathers, sons, and husbands to help run farms, businesses, and households. But daily life for people in the South could be a terrible struggle.

WORDS 2 KNOW

total war: completely destroying an enemy's means of fighting a war.

The vast majority of battles were fought in the southern states. Thousands of troops moved through large areas of the South and civilians there provided the food, shelter, and supplies they needed. As the war years went by, more and more of the South was retaken by the Union. The Union policy of "**total war**" meant that many parts of the South were severely damaged, with livestock slaughtered and crops and fields ruined.

WORDS 2 KNOW

blockade: to block off a place or area.

riot: to protest something in a violent way.

The biggest problem for people in the South was the shortage of food. Union troops **blockaded** the cities to keep food and supplies from reaching them. Part of the problem was that before the war, most of the land in the South had been devoted to growing cotton, not food crops. The people of Richmond, Virginia, suffered from such severe food shortages that in the spring of 1863, women **rioted** in what became known as the Richmond Bread Riots.

Another major shortage in the Confederate states was fabric. Although the southern states produced most of the cotton used to make cloth in the United States before the war, the textile mills were in the Union states. Many southern women learned how to sew, knit, and spin for the first time, since wealthy families had always relied on slaves to do this kind of work. "Homespun" dresses, made from cotton spun and sewed by hand, became common.

Burned out section of Richmond, Virginia.

In both the North and the South, the war allowed many women to take on roles outside their traditional ones as mothers, daughters, and wives. Women supported the war effort in many ways. They participated in Ladies' Aid Societies, were nurses, acted as spies, and a few even disguised themselves as men and became soldiers. Many women took over the male roles in their households, including overseeing plantations and farms and running businesses.

Despite the overwhelming hardships of life in wartime, people still had fun, held parties and dances, and lived their day-to-day lives as best they could. Band concerts and traveling circuses were a popular form of live entertainment during the Civil War. Children learned with dolls and wooden toys, and played a new game that became incredibly popular throughout the North and South: baseball.

WORDS 2 KNOW

influx: the arrival of large numbers of people.

When the war officially ended in 1865 and the southern states rejoined the Union, life in the United States was forever changed. Slaves who had never known independence were able to start their lives anew as free people. Southerners rebuilt their homes, lives, and land, without the benefit of slave labor. Northerners had to adapt to a postwar economy and the **influx** of thousands of men who were returning to a workforce that wasn't ready for them.

Families had to adjust to being together again with men who had lived through terrible experiences.

Outside the city of Atlanta, Georgia.

BERRY INK & HOMEMADE PAPER

Resources of all kinds—food, fuel, clothing, and shoes—were in short supply as the Civil War dragged on, especially in the South. The hardest hit were the southern poor. Many basic household items that were previously manufactured in the North and shipped south were no longer available. Even simple things like writing a letter took some creativity.

The main form of communication between families and soldiers was through letter writing, and it was also a way for many soldiers to pass time at camp. Receiving a letter from home was the highlight of the day for most soldiers.

Soldiers had to buy their own paper, pens, and stamps to write and send letters. Later in the war, organizations such as the U.S. Christian Commission and U.S. Sanitary Commission gave out paper and envelopes to soldiers free of charge.

In 1864, the U.S. Mail Service announced that Union soldiers could send their letters home for free as long as they wrote "soldier's letter" on the outside of the envelope. The Confederates were not able to offer that service, and shortages of paper, stamps, and even something to write with became much worse as the war dragged on.

Crowd outside the headquarters of the U.S. Christian Commission, Richmond, Virginia.

But people did not let the shortages of supplies stop them from staying in touch with their friends and relatives. They created ink from the juice of berries. When they ran out of stationery, they used any scraps of paper they could find.

∽ CIVIL WAR FACTS & TRIVIA ∾

★ Because mail delivery did not take place on a regular basis, soldiers often sent home six or more letters at a time. They numbered each letter so their families could read them in the order they were written.

★ When the Civil War began, the Confederates had to create their own postal system and mail routes. Most of the mail during that time was transported via steamboats along the rivers, and then carried over land by stagecoach or a rider on a horse.

★ Confederate postage stamps were not available after June 1, 1861, so postmasters would often write "paid," or the postage due, on the envelope. Postage was 5¢ for letters weighing less than half an ounce and sent distances less than 500 miles. Letters weighing more than a half ounce or sent distances more than 500 miles cost 10¢.

HANDMADE PAPER

Here's a great way to make your own writing paper using recycled material.

1 Soak several sheets worth of torn paper pieces in warm water for at least 30 minutes or overnight.

2 Have an adult help you bend the wire hanger to make a square-shaped frame. Cover your hanger with a nylon stocking and staple it in place to make a screen.

3 Fill the blender halfway with warm water, then add a handful of the soaked paper. Making sure the lid is on tight, blend into a pulp at medium speed until you no longer see pieces of paper. The pulp will have a soupy consistency. Make several batches. You can blend in bits of construction paper for color.

4 Pour the blended mixture into the large tub and fill it with enough warm water to cover the mixture. Stir thoroughly until the ingredients are evenly dispersed. You can stir in short pieces of thread, dried flowers, or herbs for texture.

5 Slide your frame into the tub, allowing some pulp to settle onto the screen. Hold the frame underwater, and gently move it back and forth to get an even layer of fibers on the screen.

SUPPLIES

- **scrap paper** such as paper towels, construction paper, and tissue paper torn into 1-by-1-inch pieces (2½ by 2½ centimeters)
- **2 large tubs or pots,** with one larger than the frame you use to make the paper
- **water**
- **wire clothes hanger** for frame
- **old nylon stocking**
- **stapler**
- **blender**
- **pieces of colored construction paper, colored thread, or dried flowers or herbs** (optional)
- **sponge**
- **dishtowels, felt, or newspaper** for blotting
- **rolling pin**
- **strainer**
- **iron**

6 Lift the frame out of the mixture, keeping it flat. Allow it to drip over the tub until most of the water has drained through. You should have an even layer of the pulp mixture on the screen. Press the pulp gently with your hand to squeeze out excess moisture. Soak up excess water from the bottom of the screen with a sponge.

7 Place clean dishtowels, felt, or newspaper on a flat surface and flip the screen, paper-side-down, onto the cloth. Lift the screen gently, leaving behind the paper. This is called couching.

8 Cover the paper with another cloth or piece of felt, and squeeze out moisture using a rolling pin. Remove the damp cloth or felt. Make as many sheets as you like, then place the sheets out of the way to dry overnight.

9 When you're finished making paper, collect the leftover pulp in a strainer and throw it out, or freeze it in a plastic bag for future use. Never pour the pulp down the drain, because it will clog your pipes.

10 When the paper is mostly dry, you can use an iron at a medium heat setting to fully dry it. Have an adult help with the iron! When the paper is dry, pull the cloth gently from both ends, stretching it to loosen the paper. Gently peel the paper from the cloth.

ON THE HOMEFRONT
CIVIL WAR QUILTS

Although most women weren't fighting on the battlefield during the Civil War, they played an important role supporting the troops and managing things back home. As the men left to fight, women struggled to keep farms going and businesses surviving, and to feed and clothe their families. It was most difficult for women on small farms who relied on everyone in the family for help.

WORDS 2 KNOW

fundraising: an activity to earn money for a cause.

bazaar: a sale of goods for charity.

Underground Railroad: a network of houses and safe places that runaway slaves went to, from one to the next, on the way north to freedom.

Mary Tippee, sutler with Collis Zouaves, One Hundred and Fourteenth Pennsylvania Infantry.

How did communities help each other? When times were particularly tough, communities in the South created **fundraising** quilts. These were made of donated cloth scraps and pieced together by a church group or at a community quilting bee. The quilts were then sold at church **bazaars** to raise money for families who needed it most.

The Bonnet Brigades

When war broke out in 1861, the first Ladies' Aid societies sprang up all over the northern states. Women organized themselves into what were called "bonnet brigades" to provide soldiers with supplies, from bandages and food to clothes. The Ladies' Aid societies were well-organized and full of well-meaning and enthusiastic volunteers. But because they were run by individual groups of women throughout the North, their efforts weren't very well-coordinated. Some troops got far too many supplies. Others didn't get any supplies. Sometimes the supplies spoiled before they reached the soldiers or were unusable. To control the quality and quantity of supplies reaching the troops, the U.S. Sanitary Commission was formed in 1862. It distributed all supplies to the Union army and inspected camps and hospitals for the North. Many women volunteered to be part of the U.S. Sanitary Commission.

Field relief wagons and workers of the U.S. Sanitary Commission, Washington, D.C.

In the North, abolitionists held Abolitionist Fairs. Women who supported the anti-slavery cause donated quilts and other needlework to be sold to raise money for the abolitionists. These quilts often had anti-slavery poems and sayings stitched on them.

One of the most common quilt patterns during the Civil War was called Jacob's Ladder, or Four Patch, because it was made up of small squares sewn together to look like the steps of a ladder. This pattern later became known as the **Underground Railroad**, because of stories told after the war about how quilts directed runaway slaves to the path of freedom via the Underground Railroad.

The South had its own groups of Ladies' Aid societies. These volunteers banded together to support their husbands, sons, and brothers on the battlefield.

At the beginning of the war, what the Confederates needed most was gunboats. Southern Ladies' Aid societies enthusiastically supported the Confederate cause by making gunboat quilts that they sold or raffled off to raise money. By the end of 1862, enough money had been raised to buy three gunboats. Unfortunately, by this time the Confederate navy had suffered so many defeats, their seaports were about to fall to the Union.

Southern Ladies' Aid societies then turned their skills to supporting the troops, and they spent much of their energy supplying clothing and bedding.

∾ CIVIL WAR FACTS & TRIVIA ∾

★ Quilts made for soldiers during the Civil War often had inspiring words stitched on them to encourage the soldiers on the battlefield. Many soldiers wrote to the women who made them, thanking them for their quilts. This led to letter-writing exchanges between soldiers and single women, and some soldiers married the women who made quilts for them.

WORDS 2 KNOW

petition: a written request signed by many people.

★ Female anti-slavery societies were founded by white and free black women in the northern states many years before the Civil War. They raised money for their cause, opened schools for black children, and passed around **petitions** to raise awareness about the evils of slavery.

FOUR PATCH QUILT BLOCK

strips of material 2½ inches wide, 2 different colors

Color 1

Color 2

SUPPLIES

- **2 different colored fabrics** one light and one dark, ½ yard of each (about ½ meter)
- **ruler** or measuring tape
- **scissors**
- **pins, needle, thread**
- **iron**

1 Cut two, 2½-inch-wide strips of each fabric (6¼ centimeters). Place the light strip on top of the dark strip, with the more colorful sides of the fabric facing together. This is known as "right sides together." Pin and then stitch the dark strip to the light strip along one of the long edges with a ¼-inch seam allowance (½ centimeter). This is the distance between the line that you're sewing and the edge of the fabric. It is the width of all the seams in this project.

2 Once you've sewn the two strips together, measure and cut ten, 2½-inch-wide pieces from your long strip (6¼ centimeters). Then open each piece up and lay two pieces on top of one another, right sides together. Stitch two pieces together so that the dark fabric and light fabric are opposite each other, like a checkerboard. Make five of these four-patch blocks. They will be approximately 4½ inches square (11¼ centimeters square).

cut 2½ inches squares from strips sewn together

make 5 of these

3 Cut two, 4⅞-inch squares of each color fabric, dark and light (12¼ centimeters). Cut each square in half diagonally and sew one dark triangle to one light triangle to make a square. When you're done you'll have four, 4½-inch squares made up of dark and light triangles (11¼ centimeters square).

make 4 of these

CONTINUES ON NEXT PAGE . . .

4 Have an adult help you with this step. If you iron your blocks flat the next stage will be easier. Iron the sides with the seams first, ironing the seams open. Then iron the right side.

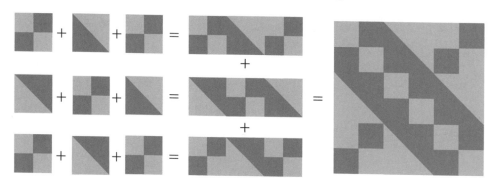

5 Line up your four-patch blocks and your triangle blocks in the pattern shown above. Put the middle patch of the first row on top of the first patch in that row, with right sides together. Pin and sew down the right side. Open up the fabric, and place the third patch in the first row on top of the second patch in that row, right sides together, and sew down the right side. Do the same for the other two rows you've laid out in a pattern. When you're done you'll have three strips of three squares sewn together. Iron all the seams open.

6 Now take the top strip and place it on the middle strip, right sides together. Pin the strips in place along the top edge. (Open it up to check that you have the correct edges pinned before you stitch.) Sew one long seam across the entire length of the two strips. Open up the fabric, and place the bottom strip of squares on the middle strip, right sides together. Pin the strips together along the bottom edge (open it up to check). Sew one long seam across the entire length of these two strips.

7 Open up the fabric, and you will have a nine-patch quilt square! Use the iron again to press your square for a nice, finished look.

PILLOW OR WALL HANGING

You can easily make your four patch quilt square into a finished pillow or wall hanging.

1 Cut a square out of the fabric measuring 12½ inches by 12½ inches (32 centimeters square). Lay it on a work surface with the right side up. Lay your quilt square on top of the fabric square with the right side down (so right sides are together). Pin completely around three of the sides, and one quarter of the way from each corner on the fourth side. If any of the edges don't line up well you can trim a bit to make them even. Stitch these seams together leaving a ¼-inch seam allowance (½ centimeter).

2 Turn the pillowcase right side out so that the seams are on the inside. Press with the iron, pushing the seam allowance at the open gap to the inside. If you are making a wall hanging, stitch the gap closed. For a pillow, stuff the case with pillow stuffing and then sew the gap closed.

SUPPLIES

- ½ yard of fabric (about ½ meter)
- scissors
- finished four patch quilt square
- pins, needle, thread
- iron
- pillow stuffing

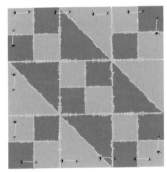

Pin back of quilt square to backing material

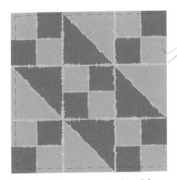

Sew quilt square to backing leaving gap unsewn

*D*uring the Civil War era, most American children played with dolls that were simple. They were often handmade by family members using supplies that were close at hand. Depending on where in the country they lived, this meant that dolls were made of wood, rags, or corn husks.

The most common doll made for little girls during the mid-1800s was the rag doll. These were popular in both the North and the South, and there were many different ways to make them. In the South, rag dolls were often called hankie dolls or plantation dolls. Rag dolls were made out of cotton fabric with cotton stuffing for its head. Sometimes they were called church dolls, since the soft cotton wouldn't make a lot of noise if they fell on the floor during church.

Rag doll found in the room where Confederate General Robert E. Lee surrendered to Union General Ulysses S. Grant.

One variation of the rag doll was called a "sugar baby." Mothers would make a rag doll and put sugar cubes in the head for their young children to suck on.

Another very common doll made by families in the Civil War was the corn husk doll. Corn was a crop grown in many parts of the country, and corn husks were plentiful. Depending on what color hair a girl wanted for her doll, she would take silk off the corn ears in the early, mid, or late season. Early-season corn held yellow silk, mid-season corn silk was reddish brown, and late-season silk was darker brown.

The "Silent Witness" Doll

One particular rag doll played a famous role in the surrender of General Robert E. Lee to General Ulysses S. Grant at Appomattox Court House on April 9, 1865. The two generals met in a house owned by a man named Wilmer McLean. He had a daughter named Lula who was playing with a rag doll in the room where

McLean house. Appomattox Court House, Virginia.

the two generals were to meet and sign the conditions of surrender. When Lula saw soldiers come into the house, she ran outside, leaving the doll behind. The doll was the "silent witness" to the surrender. When Lee left to tell his troops of the surrender, a Union soldier (Lieutenant Colonel Thomas W. C. Moore) picked up the rag doll and took it with him.

CORN HUSK DOLL

SUPPLIES

- **corn husks** (green corn husks are best—if you don't have any you can buy both green and dried husks in packages at local craft stores)
- **large bowl** filled with warm water
- **string**
- **scissors**
- **food coloring, coffee, or tea**

1 If you are using green husks, skip this step. If you are using dried husks, soak them in water until they are flexible. While the husks are soaking, cut a half dozen pieces of string, each about 5 inches in length (13 centimeters).

2 Grab several large corn husks from the bowl and tie them together an inch or two down from one end (2½– 5 centimeters). Pull the lengths of the husk down over what is to be the head part, like peeling a banana. Shape the head and tie string around what is to be the neck.

3 To make the doll's arms, remove three more husks from the bowl. Tie them together at one end, braid them together, and tie off. Cut the ends to make them even. Place the arms between the lengths of husk, then tie a piece of string around the doll's waist.

4 Crisscross thin strips of corn husk around the doll's chest, waist, and neck. Tuck the ends in (you can tie off the husk strips before tucking them in). Use thin husk strips to cover the strings at the doll's "wrists."

5 To fill out her skirt, trim the widest corn husks you have so they are approximately the same length. Wrap these husks around her middle and tie in place. Wrap her middle with a strip of husk, then trim the bottom of her skirt so it's even.

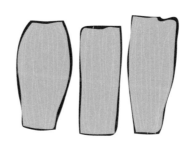

6 For hair, you can glue on dried corn silk, or take a large rectangular piece of husk, fold it, and tie it as a head scarf.

7 It's a good idea to let the doll dry, standing, on a flat surface.

Note: Corn husks can be soaked in food coloring to make colored clothing or skin. Soak husks for 30 minutes in a large bowl containing warm water and several drops of your desired color. To make vibrant browns, soak husks in a large bowl of coffee or tea.

RAG DOLL

1 To make a pattern for your doll, fold a piece of paper in half. Use a pencil to draw the outline of half of your doll onto the paper. This way the doll will be the same on each side. It should be a fairly simple design so it's easy to cut out. Add ½ inch around your doll's outline for a seam allowance (1 centimeter).

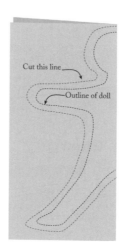

Cut this line

Outline of doll

SUPPLIES

- **craft paper** or any other medium-weight paper
- **pencils/pens**
- **scissors**
- **scrap fabric**
- **pins, thread, needle**
- **fabric paint, buttons, yarn** or whatever else you might want to decorate your doll
- **filling**—polyester fiberfill works well, but you can use any other soft, filling fabric

2 Cut the paper along the seam allowance and unfold the pattern.

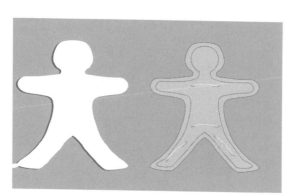

3 Place the pattern on your chosen fabric and pin it into place. Carefully cut around the pattern. Do this twice so that you have the front and back sides for your doll.

Leave gap in
seam to insert stuffing

Insert stuffing
in gap in seam

4 Decorate the front and back sides of your doll with paint if you want to. Allow the paint to dry completely before going on to the next step.

5 Pin the two sides together, with decorated sides facing each other, and carefully sew together, ½ inch from the edge of the fabric. Leave a 2-to-3-inch section open where the dolls legs meet.

6 Turn the doll right side out and stuff it with filling. When you are finished stuffing, sew the gap closed.

7 Decorate more if you'd like with yarn for hair, buttons, markers, etc.

CIVILIAN FOOD

*B*efore the start of the Civil War, most people in America had access to a variety of food. The food people ate in the 1850s and 1860s was different from what we eat today, but a lot of the staple foods are similar, such as flour, sugar, and butter. As soon as war broke out, however, food became scarce and expensive, especially for people in the South.

The Union blockaded Confederate ports, right from the beginning of the war. This made it difficult for food to reach the Confederate states by boat.

Harewood Hospital, on farm of W. W. Corcoran, Washington, D.C.
Many farms were taken over for use by the military.

Southern Food Prices

Do you think food is expensive today? Here is a list of how the price of food skyrocketed during the Civil War. To give you some perspective, gourmet coffee today is about $12 per pound, and butter is about $3 per pound.

	1861	1862	1863	1864	1865
Bacon (per pound)	13¢	75¢	$1.25–6	$8–9	$11–13
Butter (per pound)	20¢	75¢–$2	$2–4	$15–25	$15–20
Coffee (per pound)	35¢	$1.50–4	$5–30	$12–60	$72.50
Flour (per barrel)	$6.00	$16–40	$30–75	$125–500	$325–1,000

The Union army also regularly attacked Confederate towns, stealing what resources they could find. Southern cities were especially hard hit by food shortages, although rural areas also felt the devastation, as battles fought in these areas would destroy crops and other food sources.

One way people preserved their food, especially fruits and vegetables, was to dry them. Dried fruits and vegetables could be safely stored in a cool, dry place for many months. Most farmers had root cellars where they kept barrels of dried fruits and vegetables, canned foods, and salted meats. Root cellars were usually simple rooms dug directly into the ground, covered by a door. The beauty of a root cellar was that it stayed cool during the summer months, so food stored there didn't spoil in hot and humid weather.

KNOW YOUR CIVIL WAR SLANG

long sweetening—molasses.

goobers—peanuts.

Sometimes people hosted "biscuit parties," where people brought flour to make bread or biscuits for a large group. In the South, as food shortages became severe, people threw "starvation parties," where the only refreshment was water. Dances and dinners were put on for soldiers who came home from war for Christmas or other holidays. One favorite party activity was a taffy pull. People made a batch of taffy, buttered their hands, and chose partners. Then they pulled the taffy until it was light and lost its elasticity. Taffy pulls were major social events for unmarried men and women, although during the war most taffy pulls were women-only, since so many men were serving in the military.

∾ CIVIL WAR FACTS & TRIVIA ∾

★ Coffee was both the scarcest and most valued drink during the Civil War. Many people came up with interesting coffee substitutes, including okra seed, rice, wheat, peanuts, beans, sweet potatoes, peas, and acorns. These were dried and then soaked in hot water, creating a coffee-like drink.

★ Since cane sugar and molasses were produced mostly in the South, Northerners used maple sugar instead to protest against the South.

★ At the beginning of the Civil War, Northerners enjoyed scrambled eggs, tea, bread, fried fish, wild pigeon, and oysters for breakfast, while Southerners preferred fried chicken, bread with caviar, and mutton with onions. As the war went on, both groups were reduced to tea or coffee and bread for their morning meal—if that was even available.

★ During General Sherman's march to the sea from August to November 1864, his troops burned and destroyed hundreds of barns full of grain and corn that had just been harvested. Troops also killed livestock. These northern troops were called bummers because of it, and the South's recovery was very slow and difficult as a result of the destruction of basic food supplies.

MOLASSES TAFFY

Have an adult help you with this project.

1 In a heavy saucepan, combine molasses, sugar, and water.

2 Cook the mixture over low heat, stirring frequently until the thermometer reads 272 degrees Fahrenheit (133 degrees Celsius). A small amount of the mixture will crack when dropped in cold water.

3 Remove the saucepan from the heat and add butter, baking soda, and salt. Stir until the ingredients are just blended. Don't overmix.

4 Pour the mixture into a large, shallow, buttered pan and allow it to cool down enough so that you can handle it.

5 Grease your hands with butter and gather the taffy into a ball. Pull the taffy using your fingers until it is firm and light yellow in color.

6 Stretch the taffy into a long rope, twist slightly and cut with scissors into 1-inch pieces (2½ centimeters). If not eaten immediately, wrap in waxed paper. This recipe should make about four dozen pieces.

SUPPLIES

- saucepan
- stove
- **4 cups molasses** (950 milliliters)
- **1 cup brown sugar** (230 grams)
- **½ cup water** (120 milliliters)
- **stirring spoon**
- **candy thermometer**
- **4 tablespoons butter** (60 grams)
- **½ teaspoon baking soda** (2 grams)
- **⅛ teaspoon salt** (½ gram)
- **large, shallow pan**
- **extra butter** for pan and hands
- **scissors**
- **waxed paper**

FRUIT DEHYDRATOR

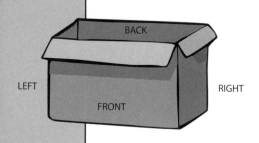

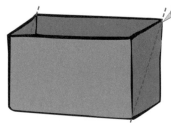

SUPPLIES

- scissors or knife
- cardboard box
- pencil
- ruler
- cheesecloth
- tape
- aluminum foil
- fresh fruit (apples, pears, grapes)
- needle
- thread
- plastic wrap
- lemon juice and water (optional)

1 Have an adult help you use the scissors or knife to carefully cut off the top of the box. Label the sides of the box, *left*, *right*, *front*, and *back*.

2 On the right and left sides of the box, use your ruler to draw a diagonal line from the top back corner to the bottom front corner. Use the scissors or knife to cut along these diagonal lines. Once the lines are cut, cut off the front of the box. This should leave you with half of a box with a triangular shape.

3 Use the pencil to draw triangular windows on the left and right sides of the box. Cut these windows out.

4 Cover the windows with cheesecloth, taping it securely to the cardboard.

5 Use the aluminum foil to cover the back, bottom and sides of the inside of your box. Make sure to leave the cheesecloth uncovered.

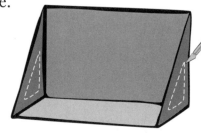

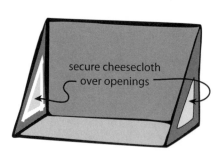

secure cheesecloth over openings

tape foil inside

6 Tape the foil securely to the inside of the box so that it won't fall off when you move the box around.

7 Slice your fruit thinly, but thick enough so that it will hang on a string without breaking. Use the needle and thread to string the pieces of fruit so that they hang with space in between each piece.

8 Cut two very small holes on either side of the box above the cheesecloth screens. Thread the string through these holes so that the fruit hangs inside the dehydrator. Place tape over the holes to hold the string in place, and so that nothing can get into the box.

9 Now that your fruit is hanging, cover the front of the box with plastic wrap. Secure it with tape, leaving the cheesecloth uncovered.

10 Dry your fruit! The best way to do this is to set the fruit out in the sun every day for three or four days. Bring it inside at night so that it doesn't get too cold or eaten by a wild animal.

Note: You may need to start with a larger quantity of fruit than you think. It shrinks down when it dries! Also, soaking the fruit in a mixture of 1 cup of lemon juice and 1 quart of water first will help prevent the fruit from browning.

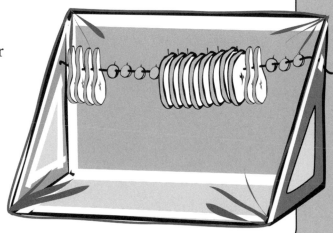

ROCK CANDY

Rock candy is another sweet that has been around since the Civil War. Depending on where they lived, people made rock candy from cane sugar, beet sugar, or maple sugar.

1 Tie one end of the piece of string around the pencil. Cut the string so it won't touch the bottom of the jar when the pencil is laid across the opening.

2 Wet the string and roll it in sugar. Lay the pencil over the top of the jar so the string hangs down inside the jar. Don't let the string stick to the jar sides.

3 Have an adult help you bring the sugar and water to a boil, stirring so that the sugar dissolves. Remove from heat as soon as it boils. Stir in the food coloring and flavor.

4 Pour the mixture into the jar. Let the sugar water sit for a few days in a sunny window. The sun will help the water evaporate faster.

5 You should start seeing crystals develop in a few hours, but let it sit for at least three days. The crystals will grow larger the longer you leave the string in the jar.

SUPPLIES

- string
- pencil
- clear glass or plastic jar
- **2 cups granulated sugar** (460 grams)
- **1 cup water** (240 milliliters)
- **pot**
- **stove**
- **food coloring**
- **candy flavoring** such as peppermint, cherry, or lemon (optional)

CIVIL WAR FASHION

Shortages of fabric and other dress goods during the Civil War meant that many women, especially those in the South, had to change the way they dressed.

Fashions in the 1860s **accentuated** a woman's waist. Most dresses featured a fitted **bodice** with wide, puffy sleeves to make the shoulders look broader. Hoop skirts made the hips look wider to showcase a tiny waist. As the war dragged on and fabric became harder to find, hoop skirts went out of fashion. Too much fabric was required to cover the hoops.

WORDS 2 KNOW

accentuate: to bring attention to something.

bodice: the part of a dress above the waist.

Fashion of the 1860s.

Women had long hair, but pinned it up, and they rarely left the house without a bonnet on. Bonnets were mostly used to frame a woman's face, rather than protect her from the sun. Bonnet fashions changed over the war years, too, with bonnets getting smaller and smaller as the years went by, eventually being replaced by small hats.

WORDS 2 KNOW

forward: behaving boldly, in ways not approved of.

decipher: to figure out the meaning of something.

Most women, especially in the South, carried fans to cool themselves off during the hot and humid months. Fans were also used for wordless communication. With different movements of the fan, a woman could give unspoken messages. This allowed her to communicate without appearing too **forward**, an undesirable trait for women in the Civil War era.

The Language of the Fan

The idea that fans can convey messages in a kind of "fan language" has been around since the eighteenth century. There are many written records for **deciphering** coded messages sent by fan. For instance, it is said that if you place your fan near your heart, it means that you love the person this gesture is directed toward. If you fan quickly, you're engaged to be married, while if you fan slowly, you are already married. Holding your fan half opened at your lips means that you would like to be kissed, and if you open and close your fan several times it means that you think the person you directed your motion toward was cruel.

One of the most popular forms of fashion during the 1860s was "**mourning** fashion." It was popularized by England's Queen Victoria. Her husband, Prince Albert, died in 1861, just as the American Civil War was beginning. Queen Victoria dressed in black mourning clothes to honor her husband. She wore mourning clothes for more than 40 years and sparked a fashion trend that jumped across the Atlantic Ocean. It coincided with a time when many American women experienced the death of a loved one.

Mourning fashion wasn't just a black dress: it included bonnets, hats, veils, handkerchiefs, shoes, and any other piece of clothing seen in public. Businesses specialized in selling only black clothing. Mourning apparel extended to jewelry, as well, with mourning jewelry usually made of **gutta-percha**. Lockets were also very much in fashion, and women often carried locks of hair given to them by their husbands, sons, or sweethearts.

WORDS 2 KNOW

mourning: to show sadness about someone's death.

gutta-percha: a substance made from tree sap that looks black when it hardens.

corset: a stiff piece of underclothing with laces tied as tight as possible to make a woman's waist looker narrow.

∽ CIVIL WAR FACTS & TRIVIA ∽

★ Clothes worn by women were quite impractical, with the long trailing skirts that were nearly impossible to keep clean.

★ Young women who wore hoop skirts were known as "tilters," because of the skirt's tendency to rise up or tilt in the back.

★ Many women campaigned for dress reform. They argued that the **corset**, which squeezed in the waist as tightly as possible, was bad for a woman's health.

FAN

1 Have an adult help you use the hammer and nail to carefully make a small hole at the end of each popsicle stick. The holes should be in about the same place on each stick.

2 Thread the embroidery floss or ribbon through the holes, creating a stack of popsicle sticks. Tie the floss or ribbon in a loose knot.

3 Create a fan shape by spreading the sticks apart. Place the sticks on the paper and trace a curved fan shape on the paper.

4 Cut out and decorate the paper—be creative!

5 Make a fold on each edge of the paper, about half an inch wide. Place the paper right-side-down, fan out the popsicle sticks, and glue them to the underside of the paper. Then glue the folds onto the outer popsicle sticks to hold the fan in place.

Allow the glue to dry, and add more decorations if you'd like.

SUPPLIES

- **hammer**
- **nail**
- **7 thick popsicle sticks**
- **embroidery floss** or thin ribbon
- **scissors**
- **poster board** or heavy construction paper
- **decorating materials** like markers, feathers, sequins, glitter
- **glue**

POPULAR MUSIC

The most popular music in America for almost 30 years before and during the Civil War was called minstrel music. This music was based on two musical traditions: African and **Celtic**. Minstrel music featured four main instruments: banjos, fiddles, tambourines, and the bones, made of two pig or cow rib bones.

WORDS 2 KNOW

Celtic: Irish and Scottish.

immigrant: a person who moves to a new country.

Banjos were brought to America by African slaves in the late 1600s, and their music became part of the culture of the South. Most of the white South was settled by Scottish and Irish **immigrants**, and they brought Celtic fiddle songs with them. From the mixture of the two musical traditions have come uniquely American music, including the blues, bluegrass, country, ragtime, and Dixieland.

Minstrel music was also based on an ugly tradition called "blackface," which had been part of American music since Colonial times. Minstrels were white people who blackened their faces, exaggerated their speech, and performed on stage while making fun of black people.

Banjo player in traditional "blackface" from a minstrel show.

Minstrel shows usually consisted of three parts. First members of the whole minstrel troupe sang popular songs and told jokes and riddles. Then a variety act included performers on stage one at a time to do separate acts. The third part was usually a skit that combined acting and songs that commented on current events.

"Bones" player.

Minstrel shows became popular in the 1840s, when a group called the Virginia Minstrels toured the country, playing music and performing skits. They were such a hit they caused a minstrel craze that peaked right around the time of the Civil War. Hundreds of minstrel groups performed in cities all over the country. Minstrel music was played by anyone who could pick up a banjo, fiddle, or bones.

Depiction of a boy with a banjo.

∽ CIVIL WAR FACTS & TRIVIA ∽

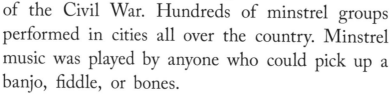

★ Plantation owners sometimes sent slaves with musical talent to New Orleans or up North to learned violin to play at parties and dances.

★ Black folk music was also called "contraband" music. It was music sung or played by slaves on southern plantations. Many Northerners heard this music for the first time during the Civil War, and incorporated its style and sound into new musical styles, such as the blues, after the war.

★ The most famous white banjo player during the Civil War was Sam Sweeney, an assistant to Confederate General J. E. B. Stuart.

TAMBOURINE

1 Using the ruler, measure two strips of cardboard or paper, each 2 inches wide by 24 inches long (5 by 60 centimeters).

2 Cut out the strips and glue them together, leaving a 1-inch tab at each end of the strips (2½ centimeters). You will now have one thick strip with a single-layer tab at either end.

3 Using your pencil, draw five rectangles on the strip, each about half an inch wide by 2 inches long (1 by 5 centimeters). They should be about 1½ inches apart (4 centimeters). Using scissors or the Xacto knife, have an adult help you cut out the rectangles. Decorate your tambourine.

4 Next, bend the strip into a circle and glue the tabs together. Use clothespins to hold the tabs together until the glue dries. If the tambourine needs to be stronger, you can glue another piece of paper or cardboard at the seam.

5 Cut off the sharp ends of your five toothpicks, and put each toothpick through two washers. If you are using bottle caps, use a hammer and nail to punch a hole through the caps and place two on each toothpick. Have an adult help you use the hot glue gun to glue the toothpicks in the center of each rectangle cut-out. Allow to dry.

SUPPLIES

- **ruler**
- **cardstock paper** or cardboard
- **scissors**
- **glue**
- **pencil**
- **Xacto knife**
- **markers** or paint
- **clothespins**
- **5 toothpicks**
- **10 bottle caps** or metal washers
- **hot glue gun**
- **hammer and nail**

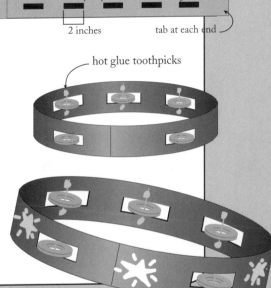

tab at each end   1½ inches

2 inches   tab at each end

hot glue toothpicks

BANJO

SUPPLIES

- **large plastic container** (2 to 4 quarts or liters)
- **scissors**
- **wood strip**, 30 by 1 by 2 inches (76 by 2½ by 5 centimeters)
- **2 nails**, 1-inch (2½ centimeters)
- **hammer**
- **2 screw eyes**
- **3 yards nylon fishing line** (3 meters)
- **2 pieces of wood**, ¾ by 2 by ¼ inch (2 by 5 by ½-centimeter)
- **saw**
- **sandpaper**

1 Cut off the top half of the plastic container. Cut flaps on opposite sides of the container about 1 inch above the bottom (2½ centimeters). The flaps should be just big enough that the wood strip fits through. Slip the wood strip through the flaps. This will be the "neck" of the banjo.

2 Hammer the nails in side by side at the very end of the neck of the banjo. Leave ¼ inch of the nails showing (½ centimeter).

nails

screw eyes

3 Screw the screw eyes into the opposite end of the neck, leaving them partially unscrewed. Tie pieces of fishing line between the nails and screw eyes. Knot them so that they are secure.

KNOW YOUR CIVIL WAR SLANG

. . . .

banjar, bangie, banza— banjo.

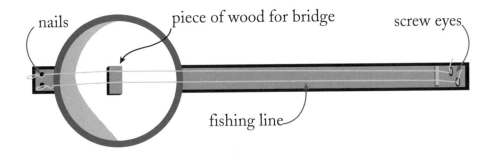

nails — piece of wood for bridge — screw eyes

fishing line

4 Take one of the smaller pieces of wood for the "bridge." Have an adult help you with the saw. Cut string-size grooves on the 2-inch side of the bridge so that the strings can sit securely on the bridge. Use sand paper to smooth the edges. Insert the bridge under the strings at the point where the strings cross the center of the bottom of the plastic container.

5 Place the other small piece of wood under the strings next to the screw eyes. This will give the strings extra tension. To tighten the strings, screw the screw eyes in tighter. The strings should be as tight as possible.

Banjo Drum

Banjos brought to America by slaves were made of gourds, wood, and tanned skins, with hemp or gut for the strings. Hemp is fiber from a plant. Gut is a cord made from animal intestines. During the Civil War, soldiers would use whatever supplies they could find to make simple banjos to play in camp. They would sometimes sneak into drummers' tents and make a hole in the head of a drum, then wait until the drummers threw out the drum head. Then they would use it for their banjos.

THE UNDERGROUND RAILROAD

The Underground Railroad started well before the Civil War began. Established around 1830, this "railroad" didn't have trains. It was a network of houses and other safe places for slaves escaping to the North. These safe places were called "stations" and guides were called "conductors."

Fugitive slaves Rappahannock, Virginia, August 1862.

Slaves learned about routes to freedom by word of mouth and through stories and songs. "Follow the Drinking Gourd" was a song that explained how to follow the North Star of the Big Dipper north, to Canada.

The Fugitive Slave Act of 1850 made it illegal for anyone to help runaway slaves. Fines and punishments were given to anyone found hiding or helping slaves escape to freedom. Slave catchers from the South traveled to northern cities to capture escaped slaves. They also kidnapped free black people and brought them back south.

The American Colonization Society

In 1816, two groups of Americans formed the American Colonization Society. One group was Southerners who wanted to keep African Americans as slaves but wanted freed slaves out of America. The other group was Northerners who wanted to free all the slaves and return them to Africa. They all believed that free African Americans could never join the white culture in America or become a significant part of society. The American Colonization Society raised money to send free blacks back to Africa, forming the colony of Liberia. In 1847, a black governor was elected, making Liberia the first nation in Africa to be governed by a black person. By 1860, about 11,000 blacks had moved to Liberia.

Slave catchers made a lot of money collecting rewards for fugitive slaves. Only a fraction of the millions of slaves in the South before the Civil War even tried to escape. Since most free blacks had little or no documentation of their free status, they were easily "caught" and resold as slaves.

Slaves in the South fought slavery by working as slowly as possible, faking sicknesses, and destroying farm equipment and machinery.

REWARD

Ran away from his Master, Maynard Reeves Bond, of Larkspur Plantation on the Edisto River, Dorchester County, South Carolina, a black fellow about 30 years of age, named Jeff, 6 Feet two inches high, wearing a brown wool jacket and denim breeches. Last seen hereabouts on October 15, 1851. Accompanying the runaway are his wife, Lavinia, age 28, and two children, Jeff, 9, and Pearl, 1. Whoever shall take up these four runaways and return them to their abovesaid Master shall have $250.00 reward. All Masters of Vessels and others are hereby cautioned against concealing or carrying off said Servants, on Penalty of the Law.

Charleston, S.C., Oct. 21, 1851.

Stations on the Underground Railroad were marked by signals to indicate whether or not the place was safe. One signal that indicated a safe stop on the Underground Railroad was a lantern hanging on a hitching post outside an established safe house. If the lantern was lit, it meant it was safe to approach. If the lantern was out, it was too dangerous to knock on the door.

Perhaps the most famous person involved in the Underground Railroad was Harriet Tubman. She was known to many runaway slaves as "Moses." Harriet Tubman was born into slavery in Maryland, escaping to Philadelphia in 1849 when she was a young woman. She worked there as a maid, and soon began helping to free other slaves through the Underground Railroad. She was one of the most wanted fugitives, and thousands of dollars was offered as a reward for

Harriet Tubman

her capture. She traveled back to the South multiple times, and in her first trip she managed to bring her sister and her sister's children back to Philadelphia with her.

Harriet Tubman (far left) with slaves she helped during the Civil War.

By the time the Civil War was over, Harriet Tubman had helped more than 50 slaves escape to freedom.

∾ CIVIL WAR FACTS & TRIVIA ∾

★ Slaves used a hollowed out gourd to scoop water out of a bucket to drink. They called the Big Dipper the Drinking Gourd.

★ The song "Follow the Drinking Gourd" gave coded directions for slaves escaping from Alabama and Mississippi, telling them to leave in the winter, where and when to cross the rivers, and where to meet guides to lead them to Canada.

RAILROAD LANTERN

1 Draw a pattern on the can with the marker.

2 Fill the empty tin can with water and freeze until solid. The ice in the can will keep it from collapsing when you make holes in it.

3 Have an adult help you use the hammer and nail. Pierce the can with the nail along the pattern lines. When you're done, the pattern you drew with the marker should be completely outlined with small nail holes. You can use different size nails to make the pattern more interesting.

4 Punch a hole at the top of the can on each side, using the hammer and nail. This is where your wire hanger will go.

5 Poke the wire through both sides of the can and twist the ends together. You'll use this to hang your lantern outside.

6 Sit the can in the sink while the ice melts. Pour out the remaining water. When the can is dry, place the tea candle in the bottom of the lantern and light it. The light from the candle will shine through the pattern, lighting the way to freedom.

SUPPLIES

- empty tin can
- black permanent marker
- water
- freezer
- hammer and nails
- 6-inch piece of wire (15 centimeters)
- tea candle

abolish: to end something.

abolitionist: someone who believed that slavery should be abolished, or ended.

accentuate: to bring attention to something.

activist: a person who fights for something they believe in.

amputate: to cut off.

artillery: a division of the army that handles large weapons.

asset: something useful or valuable.

banjar, bangie, banza: banjo.

barrack: housing for soldiers.

bazaar: a sale of goods for charity.

blockade: to block off a place or area.

bodice: the part of a dress above the waist.

bombproof: an underground shelter. Also an officer or soldier who never fought in battles.

bread basket: stomach.

Bummer: a loafer, a forager, or someone safe in the rear.

Bummer's cap: regulation fatigue or forage cap.

casualty: someone killed or injured in battle.

cavalry: soldiers trained to fight on horseback.

Celtic: Irish and Scottish.

chicken guts: officer's gold braiding on his cuff.

civilian: a person who is not a soldier.

Civil War: the war in the United States, from 1861 to 1865, between the states in the North and the slave-owning states in the South.

Confederate: the government established by the southern states of the United States after they left the Union in 1860 and 1861. Called the Confederate States of America or the Confederacy.

Constitution: the document that sets up the rules for how our country is governed.

corset: a stiff piece of underclothing with laces tied as tight as possible to make a woman's waist looker narrow.

current: the steady flow of water in one direction.

custom-made: made to exactly fit one person.

decipher: to figure out the meaning of something.

draft: a system where people have to join an army.

draft: the depth of water needed to float a ship.

duds: clothing.

evacuate: to leave a dangerous place to go to a safe place.

federal territory: land belonging to the United States that was not yet a state.

fertile: good for growing crops.

fit as a fiddle: in good shape, healthy, feeling good.

fleet: a group of ships.

flotilla: a group or fleet of ships.

forage: to search for food or provisions, and live off the land.

forces: a military group organized to fight.

forward: behaving boldly, in ways not approved of.

fresh fish: new recruits.

fugitive: someone who escapes or runs away.

fundraising: an activity to earn money for a cause.

goobers: peanuts.

grab a root: have a potato for dinner.

gray backs: southern soldiers.

gutta-percha: a substance made from tree sap that looks black when it hardens.

hayfoot, strawfoot: command used to teach new soldiers the difference between left (hayfoot) and right (strawfoot).

here's your mule: a term the infantry used to insult the cavalry.

hornets: bullets.

hospital rat: a person who fakes illness.

housewife: a sewing kit.

immigrant: a person who moves to a new country.

infantry: soldiers trained to fight on foot.

influx: the arrival of large numbers of people.

innovation: a new idea or invention.

issue: subject of concern.

jawings: talking.

long sweetening: molasses.

Louisiana Purchase: land west of the Mississippi River that the United States bought from France in 1803.

malnourishment: poorly fed or not fed enough.

mass-produce: to make large quantities of things in factories.

mess: cooking and eating food together.

messmates: soldiers who cooked and ate together.

militia: people with military training who are called up only during an emergency.

mourning: to show sadness about someone's death.

obsolete: no longer made or used.

opening of the ball: units waiting to move into battle.

pension: a regular payment made by the government after service ends.

periscope: a tube with a set of mirrors for viewing objects or people that are out of sight.

petition: a written request signed by many people.

picket: a guard or guard duty.

picket line: the line between Confederate and Union soldiers on the battlefield.

plantation: a large farm in the South with slaves for workers.

possum: a buddy.

prohibit: to make illegal.

reconnaissance: military observation to locate an enemy.

recruitment rally: a public gathering to add new members to an army.

reenactment: acting out a past event.

reenactor: someone who acts out a past event.

regiment: a large group of soldiers divided into smaller groups, called battalions.

riot: to protest something in a violent way.

sawbones: a surgeon.

screw propeller: a rod with blades that is turned by an engine to move an airplane or ship.

GLOSSARY

secede: to leave, or formally withdraw.

siege fighting: long battles where each side digs in and waits for the other side to surrender.

slavery: when slaves are used as workers. A slave is a person owned by another person and forced to work, without pay, against their will.

slave trade: buying people in Africa to sell in America.

snug as a bug: very comfortable or cozy.

somebody's darling: a dead soldier. Also the name of a popular Civil War song.

standardized: all the same.

steamboat: a boat with a paddle wheel that is turned by a steam engine. The steam generates power to run the engine.

sutler: someone who sells food and supplies to an army.

sympathizer: a person who agrees with an opinion or a side of an issue.

top rail: first class, the best.

total war: completely destroying an enemy's means of fighting a war.

trench warfare: when opposing troops fight from ditches facing each other.

troops: large groups of soldiers.

turret: a small tower for guns or other weapons.

Underground Railroad: a network of houses and safe places that runaway slaves went to, from one to the next, on the way north to freedom.

Union: the United States, but especially the northern states during the American Civil War.

vittles: food or rations.

web feet: a term the cavalry used to insult the infantry.

Zuzu: Zouaves.

PHOTO CREDITS

All images other than the ones listed here are courtesy of the Library of Congress.
Cover: Drums, courtesy of Michael K. Sorenson;
p. 12: Johnny Shiloh, *www.cs.amedd.army.mil/rlbc/clem.htm*;
pgs. 29, 30: *www.history.navy.mil*; p. 41: *www.navymedicine.med.navy.mil*;
pgs. 42, 43: *www.history.navy.mil*; p. 58: *www centennialofflight.gov*;
p. 78: letters, *www.bee.net*; pgs. 101, 102: Fashion illustrations, courtesy Son of the South, *www.sonofthesouth.net*; p. 105: banjo player, *home.versateladsl.be*.

BOOKS

- Beard, D.C. *The American Boy's Handy Book*. David Godine, 1998.

- Bolotin, Norman. *Civil War A to Z: A Young Readers' Guide to Over 100 People, Places, and Points of Importance*. Dutton Children's Books, New York, 2002.

- Brackman, Barbara. *Quilts from the Civil War*. C&T Publishing, Lafayette, California, 1997.

- Chang, Ina. *A Separate Battle: Women and the Civil War*. From *Young Readers' History of the Civil War series*. Lodestar Books, New York, 1991.

- Corrick, James A. *Life among the Soldiers and Cavalry*. The Civil War series, Lucent Books, San Diego, 2000.

- Currie, Stephen. *Women of the Civil War*. Women in History series, Lucent Books, 2003.

- Damon, Duane. *When This Cruel War Is Over: The Civil War Home Front*. Lerner Publications, Minneapolis, 1996.

- Davis, Burke. *The Civil War: Strange & Fascinating Facts*. Wings Books, New York, 1996.

- Hakim, Joy. *A History of US: War, Terrible War (Volume 6)*. Oxford University Press, 2002.

- Hesse, Karen. *A Light in the Storm: The Civil War Diary of Amelia Martin*. *Dear America series*. Scholastic, New York, 1999

- Langellier, John P. *Terrible Swift Sword: Union Artillery, Cavalry, and Infantry, 1861-1865*. Chelsea House Publishers, Philadelphia, 2002.

- Luchetti, Cathy. *Medicine Women: The Story of Early-American Women Doctors*. Crown, New York, 1998.

- McPherson, James M. *Fields of Fury: the American Civil War*. Atheneum Books for Young readers, New York, 2002.

BOOKS (CONTINUED)

- Murphy, Jim. *The Boys' War.* Clarion Books, 2002.

- O'Brien, Patrick. *Duel of the Ironclads: The* Monitor *vs. The* Virginia. Walker & Company, New York, 2003.

- Rappaport, Doreen. *No More! Stories and Songs of Slave Resistance.* Candlewick Press, Cambridge, Massachusetts, 2002.

- Roca, Steven Louis. "Presence and precedents: The USS *Red Rover* during the American Civil War, 1861-1865." *Civil War History*, July 1998.

- Varhola, Michael J. *Everyday Life During the Civil War.* Writer's Digest Books, 1999.

WEB SITES

University and Government Sites

- Civil War Index Page at Dakota State University, www.homepages.dsu.edu/jankej/civilwar/civilwar.htm

- Library of Congress Civil War Photographs, memory.loc.gov/ammem/index.html

- National Civil War Museum, www.nationalcivilwarmuseum.org

- National Park Service site (includes sections on many Civil War park sites), www.nps.gov

- United States Civil War Center, www.cwc.lsu.edu

Privately Held Sites

- www.americancivilwar.com

- www.civil-war.net

- www.teacheroz.com/civilwar.htm